THE PSYCHOSOCIAL IMPACT
OF JOB LOSS

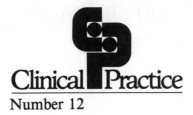

Clinical Practice
Number 12

Judith H. Gold, M.D., F.R.C.P.(C)
Series Editor

THE PSYCHOSOCIAL IMPACT OF JOB LOSS

NICK KATES, M.B.B.S., F.R.C.P.(C)
Director, East Region Mental Health Services
Associate Professor, McMaster University
Hamilton, Ontario, Canada

BARRIE S. GREIFF, M.D.
Consultant, Harvard University Health Services
Cambridge, Massachusetts

DUANE Q. HAGEN, M.D.
Chairman, Department of Psychiatry
St. John's Mercy Medical Center
St. Louis, Missouri

1400 K Street, N.W.
Washington, DC 20005

Note: The authors have worked to ensure that all information in this book concerning drug dosages, schedules, and routes of administration is accurate as of the time of publication and consistent with standards set by the U.S. Food and Drug Administration and the general medical community. As medical research and practice advance, however, therapeutic standards may change. For this reason and because human and mechanical errors sometimes occur, we recommend that readers follow the advice of a physician who is directly involved in their care or the care of a member of their family.

The paper used in this publication meets the minimum requirements of the American National Standard for Information Sciences—Permanence of Paper for Printed Library Materials, ANSI Z39.48–1984.   ∞

Library of Congress Cataloging-in-Publication Data

Kates, Nick, 1952-
    The psychosocial impact of job loss / Nick Kates, Barrie S. Greiff, Duane Q. Hagen.—1st ed.
        p.   cm.—(Clinical practice ; no 12)
    Includes bibliographical references.
    ISBN 0-88048-190-0 (alk. paper)
    1. Unemployment—Psychological aspects. I. Greiff, Barrie S. II. Hagen, Duane Q., 1935- . III. Title. IV. Series.
    [DNLM: 1. Psychology. 2. Unemployment.
    W1 CL767J no. 12 / HD 5708.5 K19p]
HD5708.K38 1990
306.3′61—dc20
DNLM/DLC
for Library of Congress   89-17955
                                                                              CIP

This book is dedicated to Alex Kates, for all his help along the way; Fishel Greiff, a mentor in regard to work; and Kit Hagen, who offers support and inspiration. The authors thank Marilyn Craven for assistance in editing this manuscript.

Contents

About the Authors

Nick Kates is the Director of East Region Mental Health Services in Hamilton, Ontario. He is an associate professor in the Department of Psychiatry at McMaster University and is the current Director of the McMaster Psychiatry Residency Program. Dr. Kates has consulted to a variety of local organizations on work-related issues and has made a number of presentations on the impact of unemployment.

Barrie S. Greiff is currently consultant to the Harvard University Health Services and a visiting professor in occupational psychiatry at the Institute of the Living in Hartford, Connecticut. He coauthored a book entitled *Tradeoffs*, which examined stress in relationships faced by company executives, and has consulted and lectured to a wide range of organizations, including IBM, General Foods, Pepsico, A. T. & T., First National Bank of Boston, and the MIT Sloan School. Dr. Greiff chairs a national committee of psychiatrists consulting to industry and is a member of the Conference Board Committee on Work and Family.

Duane Q. Hagen is Chairman of the Department of Psychiatry at St. John's Mercy Medical Center in St. Louis and has been the recipient of a National Institute of Mental Health Career Teacher's Award. He has worked full-time as a psychiatric consultant to various agencies of the federal government and has consulted to a variety of corporations, including Southwestern

Bell, A. T. & T., and McDonnell Douglas. He serves as Chairman of the American Psychiatric Association Committee on Occupational Psychiatry and was chairman of the Group for the Advancement of Psychiatry Committee on Psychiatry in Industry during the preparation of *Job Loss—A Psychiatric Perspective*, published in 1982.

Introduction
to the Clinical Practice Series

Over the years of its existence the series of monographs entitled *Clinical Insights* gradually became focused on providing current, factual, and theoretical material of interest to the clinician working outside of a hospital setting. To reflect this orientation, the name of the Series has been changed to *Clinical Practice.*

The Clinical Practice Series will provide readers with books that give the mental health clinician a practical clinical approach to a variety of psychiatric problems. These books will provide up-to-date literature reviews and emphasize the most recent treatment methods. Thus, the publications in the Series will interest clinicians working both in psychiatry and in the other mental health professions.

Each year a number of books will be published dealing with all aspects of clinical practice. In addition, from time to time when appropriate, the publications may be revised and updated. Thus, the Series will provide quick access to relevant and important areas of psychiatric practice. Some books in the Series will be authored by a person considered to be an expert in that particular area; others will be edited by such an expert who will also draw together other knowledgeable authors to produce a comprehensive overview of that topic.

Some of the books in the Clinical Practice Series will have their foundation in presentations at an annual meeting of the American Psychiatric Association. All will contain the most recently available information on the subjects discussed. Theoretical and scientific data will be applied to clinical situations, and case illustrations will be utilized in order to make the material even more relevant for the practitioner. Thus, the Clinical Practice Series should provide educational reading in a compact format especially written for the mental health clinician–psychiatrist.

Judith H. Gold, M.D., F.R.C.P.(C)
Series Editor,
Clinical Practice Series

Clinical Practice Series Titles

Treating Chronically Mentally Ill Women (#1)
Edited by Leona L. Bachrach, Ph.D., and Carol C. Nadelson, M.D.

Divorce as a Developmental Process (#2)
Edited by Judith H. Gold, M.D., F.R.C.P.(C)

Family Violence: Emerging Issues of a National Crisis (#3)
Edited by Leah J. Dickstein, M.D., and Carol C. Nadelson, M.D.

Anxiety and Depressive Disorders in the Medical Patient (#4)
By Leonard R. Derogatis, Ph.D., and Thomas N. Wise, M.D.

Anxiety: New Findings for the Clinician (#5)
Edited by Peter Roy-Byrne, M.D.

The Neuroleptic Malignant Syndrome and Related Conditions (#6)
By Arthur Lazarus, M.D., Stephan C. Mann, M.D., and Stanley N. Caroff, M.D.

Juvenile Homicide (#7)
Edited by Elissa P. Benedek, M.D., and Dewey G. Cornell, Ph.D.

Measuring Mental Illness: Psychometric Assessment for Clinicians (#8)
Edited by Scott Wetzler, Ph.D.

Family Involvement in Treatment of the Frail Elderly (#9)
Edited by Marion Zucker Goldstein, M.D.

Psychiatric Care of Migrants: A Clinical Guide (#10)
By Joseph J. Westermeyer, M.D., M.P.H., Ph.D.

Office Treatment of Schizophrenia (#11)
Edited by Mary V. Seeman, M.D., F.R.C.P.(C), and Stanley E. Greben, M.D., F.R.C.P.(C)

The Psychosocial Impact of Job Loss (#12)
By Nick Kates, M.B.B.S., F.R.C.P.(C), Barrie S. Greiff, M.D., and Duane Q. Hagen, M.D.

New Perspectives on Narcissism (#13)
Edited by Eric M. Plakun, M.D.

Preface

We have written this book because we strongly believe that a meaningful job is essential for the dignity and self-worth of an individual and his or her family.

The major restructuring of North American industry, associated with new technologies, mergers, and acquisitions, and the emergence of global competition will have a profound impact on job security and tenure over the coming decade.

We are concerned about the lack of scientific study regarding the biopsychosocial consequences of job loss and the few attempts that have been made to apply current knowledge to clinical, community, and political interventions. It is our hope that this book will catalyze a number of our colleagues, as well as those in government, industry, and organized labor, to deal with the issues of job loss in a more constructive and productive fashion.

Chapter 1

Introduction

Chapter 1

Introduction

> I thought I'd get a job in a couple of weeks, but now it's
> a couple of years. That's frightening, my confidence is
> going. When you're unemployed you feel like you've
> committed a crime somewhere but nobody tells you
> what you've done. Sometimes I think I'll go barmy. Of
> course you get depressed, you convince yourself it's
> you. Sometimes I feel really ashamed.
> Unemployed machinist, quoted in Beatrix Campbell
> *Wigan Pier Revisited*

*T*wo out of every three North Americans will lose a job at
some time during their life (Ohio State Lantern 1988). For
some the effects will be minimal, particularly if they possess
marketable skills or live in areas where there are plentiful work
opportunities. For others, such as those with a strong emotional investment in their work or with limited financial
resources, being unemployed may have a major impact on activities, relationships, and physical and emotional well-being.

While every generation has been faced with people who
were unable to find work, the forces that create unemployment
have varied. In the 1930s, one of the factors contributing to the
economic depression was an excess of supply and production
over demand. In the mid-1970s unemployment rates rose as
the "baby boom" generation began to enter the work force in
large numbers and returning Vietnam veterans joined those
looking for work. The world-wide economic recession at the
end of the 1970s led to dramatic reductions in the size of the
work force in many major industries. And in the latter part of
the 1980s, company mergers, hostile takeovers, new technologies, obsolescent industries, global competition, and the
elimination of international trade tariffs are each contributing
to the disappearance of jobs.

3

The types of problems faced by the unemployed and the way these problems present have also varied. Before World War II the attention of communities centered upon the economic deprivation and ensuing problems such as starvation and poor nutrition that threatened physical survival. Today, most Western societies have welfare systems in place that provide some degree of material assistance to unemployed individuals. Consequently, more attention is being focused on the psychological impact of job loss on workers and their families.

The increase in interest in the emotional consequences of losing a job also reflects a heightened appreciation of what a job can mean. Work and working fill a central role in our lives, meeting a multitude of emotional, social, and psychological needs. In addition to the remuneration, which helps individuals provide for themselves and their families, a job can engender a sense of purpose and value, offer opportunities for social contacts, and shape a person's identity and self-esteem.

To lose a job, or to be excluded from the work force, can erode self-confidence and create practical difficulties that can be overwhelming. Some people who lose their job find alternative work quickly, with little disruption to their daily routine. For others, continuing joblessness can lead to a sense of isolation and alienation and eventually to a state of helplessness and despair. Whatever the duration of the period of unemployment, those individuals who lose their job may develop physical and psychological symptoms of varying degrees of severity. Not all of these individuals will come into contact with psychiatric services, however, and many may not even recognize the connection between their symptoms and the loss of their job.

The effects of losing a job are complex and can affect every aspect of a person's life. While there is substantial evidence of an association between job loss and emotional and social problems, the nature of this link is complicated. Losing a job is stressful in itself but can also set in motion a train of biological, psychosocial, and family changes that can lead to further difficulties.

These complex effects are reflected in one of the recurring

questions in the debate about the impact of unemployment: Does losing a job create new problems, exacerbate preexisting difficulties and expose the problems of those individuals who are already vulnerable, or lead to multiple life adjustments that themselves become sources of further stress? Many individuals who lose their job may already be struggling to cope with personal or family difficulties, while preexisting social disadvantages can increase the likelihood of losing a job or create additional obstacles to reentry into the work force. Clearly this is not an either/or issue. Unemployment can be a predisposing, precipitating, or perpetuating factor in the onset of mental health problems, and these different effects often overlap. Trying to establish causal relationships is often complicated but may be necessary if psychiatric services are to be able to intervene effectively with those in distress.

An appreciation of the role unemployment can play in the onset of psychological problems needs to be accompanied by a recognition of the socioeconomic factors that can contribute to the loss of a job. Plant closures, economic recessions, technological advances, global competition, new styles of work, and changing social relationships can all lead to a loss of jobs.

In most industrialized countries, unemployment rates in the late 1980s are significantly lower than at the start of the decade, although in many of these countries rates are once again beginning to rise. Communities are better equipped to cope with some of the more immediate problems of the unemployed, and less public attention is focused on the problem. There are also changes in the characteristics of the unemployed as a group, with a gradual increase in the percentage of unemployed who have been out of work for more than a year—the long-term unemployed (U.S. Department of Labor 1988a).

But government-produced unemployment statistics may tell only half the story because these figures often exclude those individuals who are not actively seeking work or are looking for part-time jobs. Up to half of those who are out of work may not be accounted for in official unemployment statistics (People's Commission on Unemployment 1978). In other words, while the official unemployment rate in the United States in October 1988 was 5.5% (U.S. Department of Labor 1988b), as many as 10% of the adult population, or over 15 million potentially employable Americans, were out of work. Governments, communities, employers, organized labor, and health services need to continue to address the plight of these individuals and recognize the benefits that can result from a return to work. Unemployment is a major cause of hardship and emotional distress for millions of North Americans.

Helping the unemployed presents many challenges for psychiatrists and mental health workers who need to understand the complexities of the ways in which unemployment can affect an individual or his or her family. These challenges include an appreciation of the meaning a job can have, of the way the effects of unemployment change over time, and of the relationships between work, family, and social activities. The therapist must be able to take a systemic or ecological view of the impact of losing a job, respecting the uniqueness of the problems an individual faces, while being aware of common issues that may affect all jobless people. He or she must be aware of appropriate community resources and develop new skills in history taking, working in nontraditional treatment settings, and collaborating with social agencies. The therapist also must recognize local social and political realities that can hinder the development of necessary programs or the social reintegration of those individuals who have been out of work for lengthy periods of time. The challenges are great, yet the importance of the problem makes it one we should not overlook.

This book attempts to integrate the empirical findings of researchers who have examined the impact of unemployment with the experiences of mental health professionals who treat individuals who have lost their job. We begin, in Chapter 2, by examining the wider context within which unemployment occurs and jobs disappear. Chapter 3 reviews the evidence of previous studies concerning the psychosocial impact of unemployment, identifying some of the common issues and recurring themes in the findings.

In Chapter 4 we integrate these findings into a model that outlines how the stresses of losing a job can affect an individual, and identify the key variables that are most likely to affect the outcome of a period of unemployment. Chapter 5 demonstrates how this model can be applied to clinical situations, providing guidelines for the assessment of the problems encountered by both those individuals who have recently lost their job (job loss) and those who have been without work for a continuing period of time (unemployment).

Chapter 6 presents a comprehensive range of intervention strategies, and Chapter 7 describes how this approach has been applied to specific cases. Chapter 8 addresses questions of social policy and future research directions and discusses ways in which psychiatry as a discipline can bring its understanding of the human costs of unemployment to a public debate that frequently reduces human suffering to impersonal statistics. The final chapter summarizes the key issues in understanding the impact of job loss.

Underlying the discussion of the impact of job loss is a closely connected issue that may have even greater long-term significance, namely, the changing nature of work itself. Over the next decade technological advances, economic fluctuations, and new social relationships will have a profound effect on how work is organized, but little attention is currently being focused on the personal and societal adjustments that could be required. Comprehensive strategies must be developed to plan for these changes and to attempt to control our future rather than responding in a disorganized manner as each crisis arrives. Psychiatry can play an active role in stimulating this debate and in drawing attention to the aspects of these changes on which we are well qualified to comment.

Throughout this book six themes will recur:

The meaning of an individual's job. Working can meet many different psychological and social needs as well as economic needs. It can provide friendship and support, as well as opportunities for gaining recognition and developing compe-

7

tence, and can help young people separate from their families and enter the adult world. Understanding the functions of work helps a therapist appreciate what may have been lost when a job ended.

The interdependence of an individual's work, family, and social life. An individual's work, family, social supports, and community environment all interact, and changes in one can affect every other one as well as have an impact on psychological well-being. Effective interventions need to be based upon a systemic or ecological view of the origins and sequelae of unemployment. These interventions should be aimed at different parts of the systems in which individuals play a role, such as their family, their social support network, their workplace, or their community.

The multiple factors that can affect the impact of a period of unemployment. Many factors can contribute to the impact of the loss of a job. Some, such as social support, may minimize the effects, while others, such as insufficient finances, may amplify them. These factors are often interconnected, and their impact needs to be taken into consideration before planning an intervention strategy.

The multiple roles that psychiatric services can play. It is essential for psychiatric services to recognize that they may have multiple roles when working with the unemployed. Indeed, in many situations traditional treatments such as medication or psychotherapy may have very limited application. Other approaches such as consultation and support for other caretakers, preventive interventions in the workplace, community programs, and attempts to influence social policy may be more relevant and effective. These multiple roles highlight the importance of psychiatric services developing links and working collaboratively with other community services and agencies that may have greater day-to-day contact with the unemployed.

The importance of integrating different conceptual models. The aim of this book is not to espouse any one particular theory or hypothesis as to the impact of unemployment, but to present a unifying framework for integrating the current evidence and common mechanisms. Previous studies and writings have contributed pieces to this puzzle. We will attempt to put them together in a way that will help clinicians appraise and synthesize the existing evidence and will provide them with a means to intervene effectively when dealing with the problems of people who are out of work. Areas in which further research is required will also be identified.

The uniqueness of the experience of each individual who loses a job. The recognition of common issues or patterns must not lead us to overlook the uniqueness of the experience of each unemployed individual. Achieving this awareness requires a nonjudgmental approach that aims at understanding the patient's view of the world and takes into consideration his or her personality style, social circumstances, the manner in which the job was lost, and relevant contextual factors. The degree to which the loss of the job created new problems, exposed existing problems, or set up circumstances that in turn led to problems developing must also be borne in mind.

Before addressing these issues, we need to begin by examining the changing social and economic contexts that contribute to unemployment and the problems of jobless workers.

References

Ohio State Lantern, Aug 11, 1988, A10

People's Commission on Unemployment in Newfoundland and Labrador: Now That We've Burned Our Boats. St. John's, Newfoundland, Newfoundland and Labrador Federation of Labour, 1978

U.S. Department of Labor, Bureau of Labor Statistics: Duration of unemployment, monthly data seasonally adjusted (table). Monthly Labor Rev 111(8):69, 1988a

U.S. Department of Labor, Bureau of Labor Statistics: Employment status of the total population, data seasonally adjusted (table). Monthly Labor Rev 111(10):63, 1988b

Chapter 2

Social and Economic Context of Unemployment

Chapter 2

Social and Economic Context of Unemployment

> Distribute the earth as you will, the principal question remains inexorable. Who is to dig it? Which of us is to do the hard and dirty work for the rest and for what pay?
>
> John Ruskin "Sesame and Lilies"

*T*he last 10 years have seen dramatic fluctuations in patterns of unemployment. Prior to the economic recession of the late 1970s, Canada and the United States had grown accustomed to post-war unemployment levels of less than 7%, while the rate in most other industrialized countries was even lower. As a pressing social issue, unemployment received little attention from politicians or social scientists and even less from psychiatrists and other health workers.

The situation changed dramatically in the early 1980s, when world-wide recession and rapidly increasing rates of inflation created economic crises in most industrialized countries. Higher levels of unemployment were seen as an acceptable solution—or a necessary evil—to control inflation and reduce production costs. As a result large numbers of workers lost their jobs over a short period of time. Between 1980 and 1983 the unemployment rate in Canada rose from 7.5% to 11.9% (Statistics Canada 1983); in the United States, from 7.0% to 9.5% (U.S. Department of Labor 1988) (see Figure 2–1); and in the United Kingdom, from 7.1% to 11.9%. There were similar rises in the unemployment rate in most other industrialized countries during this period.

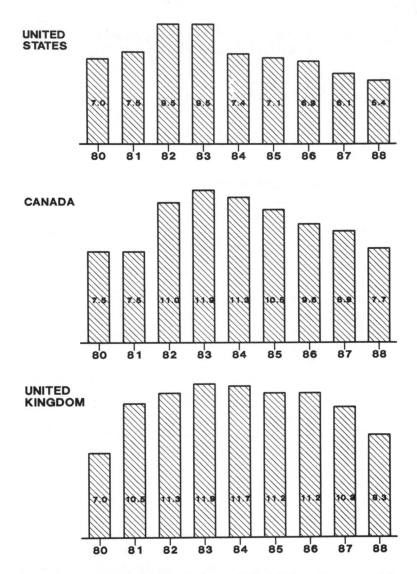

FIGURE 2–1. Unemployment rate in the United States, Canada, and the United Kingdom, 1980–1988. Source: U.S. Bureau of Labor Statistics: Annual data: employment status of the civilian working age population; 10 countries (table). Monthly Labor Review 112(6):92, 1989.

As unemployment rates crept higher, more and more people who had previously taken for granted the security their job provided found themselves out of work. In many instances losing a job was a totally unexpected experience for which individuals were ill-prepared emotionally and/or economically. At the same time general uncertainty as to how high levels of unemployment would climb created a climate of anxiety among those who were still employed.

The ranks of the unemployed were swelled by an increased number of more highly skilled and better trained workers who were faced with fewer job vacancies and greater competition for positions that were available. Entire communities were threatened, especially those that depended upon a single industry or employer. Industries that manufactured products that were less in demand (such as petroleum) or that could be produced more cheaply elsewhere (such as steel) had to make major reductions in the size of their work force.

Communities were often poorly prepared to cope with the problems faced by the unemployed. Support services were not in place, job retraining or relocation programs did not exist, and community workers had a limited understanding of the impact of unemployment and how best to intervene.

Now, at the end of the 1980s, the situation is different. Most Western countries have been able to reduce unemployment to less than 8%, and most of the more highly skilled, more mobile, or better prepared unemployed have found new jobs. Communities have developed support services, and a greater emphasis has been placed on retraining programs, although many of these have been of only limited longer-term advantage for participants. Although unemployment is still perceived as an important social issue, it appears to be less of a priority than five years ago. Indeed, some governments now appear to be concerned about sharp drops in the unemployment rate, believing that these could lead to further episodes of inflation.

Today's "unemployed" are not, however, a homogeneous group. They include individuals from different backgrounds,

15

out of work for a variety of reasons, who are coping with their predicament with varying degrees of success. Among their number are a high proportion of individuals with additional social disadvantages such as illiteracy, poverty, or belonging to a racial minority. The effects of being without a job also change over time. The longer-term unemployed, many of whom have become pessimistic about ever returning to work, face different problems from those individuals who manage to find new work relatively quickly.

Nor is the economic disruption of unemployment evenly distributed. Certain communities, geographic areas, and industries have been particularly hard hit and are finding it harder to adjust to the changes that have taken place. For example, in Canada in January 1989 the unemployment rate in Ontario, the industrial heartland of the country, was 5.2%, whereas in Newfoundland—a poorer province with an economy based on fishing, agriculture, and resource development—the rate was 17% (Statistics Canada 1988).

Even within individual industries there has been evidence of a regional shift in production. Many American companies have relocated manufacturing plants from traditional industrial areas such as the Northeast (often referred to as the Rust Belt) to newer, rapidly developing areas such as the South and West (the so-called Sun Belt). Reasons for relocation include cheaper regional production costs, technological advances that no longer tie an industry to a specific geographic location, declining local markets, and attempts to counter increased union activity. In a study of the regional variation in jobs lost, Howland (1988) concluded that there was an almost equal likelihood of jobs being lost as a result of plant closures in regions of high growth and low growth. The difference for the unemployed worker, however, was that more job opportunities were available in the high growth areas, thereby reducing the amount of time spent out of work.

One response to the problem of unemployment has been the creation of new jobs, although many of these are in the service sector and offer less security, lower wages, and fewer opportunities for advancement. New jobs are required not only to find work for those who have lost their jobs but also to accommodate people wishing to enter the work force.

In Louisiana, for example, the state with the highest level of unemployment in the United States, 11,000 new jobs were created between September 1987 and September 1988. It was estimated, however, that to provide work for everyone trying to enter or reenter the work force, 64,000 new jobs would have been required (New Orleans Times Picayune 1988). It is probably not coincidental that during the same period there was a net out-migration of 80,000 people from Louisiana. Moving elsewhere is one of the few options an unemployed person may have when living in an area with a continuing shortage of work.

It should also be borne in mind that government-produced unemployment statistics may not include all jobless workers. Those who are not actively looking for work or who are unable to work because of a physical or emotional disability may be excluded, as may be those who are working part-time or who have retired prematurely because they could not find full-time work. It has been estimated that the actual number of unemployed may be 50% higher than that indicated by official figures.

A study in Newfoundland, Canada, in 1976 found 25,000 Newfoundlanders who met the official definition of being unemployed (People's Commission on Unemployment 1978). A further 28,000 Newfoundlanders, however, who were not officially considered unemployed but were without work answered yes to the question "Do you want a job?"

Not only does this study provide a truer picture of the actual number of jobless, but it also contradicts the myth that those who are out of work are lazy or unwilling to work. In most cases the opposite is true. People want to work because of the central role working plays in their lives. In addition to providing financial remuneration it can create a sense of belonging and self-confidence. Most unemployed people wish to return to work and to contribute but feel increasingly alienated and isolated if they are unable to do so. Over time, being workless comes to be equated with being worthless. This lowered sense of self-worth, when combined with many of the other practical, physical, and emotional difficulties that the unemployed encounter, makes it even harder to reenter the work force.

Millions of North Americans are currently experiencing emotional hardship, increased stress, and even severe psychological problems as a direct consequence of being out of work or of having a family member out of work. But it is not only on account of the misery or demoralization that can follow the loss of a job that mental health professionals must be conscious of the impact of unemployment. We are entering an era when disparate social and economic forces are changing not only the way we work but our concept of work itself. These forces are likely to result in the displacement of large numbers of workers for varying periods of time over the next decade and need to be taken into consideration when predicting future patterns of unemployment. Four specific factors can be identified: the impact of new technology, the economic climate, the changing work roles of women, and the aging population.

Impact of Technology

Over the last 30 years technological advances, including automation and computerization, have contributed to increases in standards of living. In the United States, for example, the amount of disposable income has increased in real terms by 87% since 1950 (Levitan and Johnson 1982). These advances have also led to changes in the nature, the organization, and even the location of many jobs (Zuboff 1988). Automation and computerization have eliminated many jobs that were repetitive, boring, or potentially hazardous. However, they can also lead to situations in which workers who performed these jobs become redundant (Hunt and Hunt 1986).

It is uncertain how many jobs will eventually disappear as a result of increased automation or computerization. In the early 1980s some dire predictions were made as to the number of workers that would be displaced by robots (Ayres and Miller 1981), particularly in industries such as car manufacturing (Hunt and Hunt 1983). While jobs in this industry have been lost, they have been restricted primarily to areas such as welding and painting. And although within an industry such as car manufacturing up to 200,000 jobs may have been lost, approximately 100,000 new jobs have been created to manufacture robots and to maintain them once they are functioning.

Many of the jobs eliminated have been those that require lesser skill, while those jobs being created demand better educated and more highly skilled employees. As a result, workers with less formal education are likely to find it harder to break into the work force, and the newly created jobs will go to a smaller number of better educated workers.

The potential liberation of workers from certain kinds of work, a better educated labor force, and a shorter work week are in turn leading to changing expectations of a job. It has been estimated that in the United Kingdom, the total number of hours an individual entering the work force expects to work during his or her lifetime has been reduced from 100,000 hours to 50,000 hours over the last 20 years (Smith 1987). While most individuals still believe success in life depends on working hard (Pierson 1980), work is increasingly viewed as a source of psychosocial satisfaction as well as remuneration, and workers are more aware of the need for balance between their job and their family life.

Rather than being used as an excuse to eliminate jobs, the reduced time demands of work could provide an opportunity for exploring alternative work options, which could in turn affect the way work is organized. Examples exist of workplaces that have helped employees share jobs, take time off for personal projects, or negotiate paid leaves of absence (Best 1981; Reid 1986; Bergmann 1986). These options offer new ways of organizing work that could create jobs for people who cannot find work but who want to participate, especially if there is likely to be a reduction in the total amount of available work (Robertson 1985; Handy 1985).

Economic Climate

The unemployment rate is just one of many commonly utilized and interconnected indicators of economic activity and productivity. Most of these indicators follow a cyclical course with a natural ebb and flow, but they are also affected by marketplace forces of supply and demand and by economic policies.

There are many ways in which economic factors and policies can affect unemployment rates, directly or indirectly. The recovery from the recession of the early 1980s was achieved by a shrinking of the overall work force, with certain industries such as steel production being particularly hard hit. The priority given by a national government to combating unemployment or to pursuing "full employment" will also affect the number of people without work. Countries with plans for dealing with unemployment or with centralized job creation programs have been more successful in keeping unemployment rates low than countries that have only looked to the private sector or the marketplace for solutions (Therborn 1986).

There has also been a shift in the kind of work that is available. Many of the older manufacturing industries that until recently offered secure jobs with good pensions and benefits have reduced the size of their work force. The emerging industries, often based upon newer technologies, are less labor intensive and often require higher skills of their employees. Many of the new jobs that are being created are not in industry but are in the service sector, and these jobs often have limited security, lower pay, fewer benefits (including health insurance), and less chance for advancement.

In Canada in the first half of 1988, 194,000 new jobs were created, but the total number of blue-collar jobs actually decreased (Toronto Globe and Mail 1988). At the same time, the number of workers holding more than one job has doubled over the last 10 years, suggesting that more and more of the working poor are having to take on second jobs to meet their financial commitments. In other words, the creation of

194,000 new jobs does not necessarily mean that 194,000 more Canadians are working.

In addition, many of the newly created jobs are short-term or seasonal "turnstile" jobs that provide a limited number of weeks of employment but a sufficient number of weeks to establish a worker's eligibility to claim unemployment benefits for the remainder of the year.

All of these factors are contributing to the creation and perpetuation of a work force with two tiers. The upper tier consists of a decreasing number of secure "good" jobs, often filled by better educated workers, while the lower tier is made up of an increasing number of poorly protected "bad" jobs. This differentiation is being accentuated by the effects of automation and could lead to a situation in which fewer workers will receive a greater proportion of the available remuneration and benefits (Pierson 1980; Novick 1986).

This differentiation of workers could lead to a shift in the pattern of unemployment from being cyclical to becoming increasingly structural (Pierson 1980). In cyclical unemployment most industries and employees are periodically at risk because of fluctuations or downturns in the economy and changing market conditions. In contrast, structural unemployment refers to situations in which those workers with less security and fewer skills are the most vulnerable to economic downturns, irrespective of the nature of their employment. This kind of unemployment is most likely to be found in the private sector, in poorer or more isolated geographic areas, and at times of economic prosperity. Cyclical unemployment is most likely to affect white males, whereas structural unemployment has its greatest impact on women, blacks, minorities, and the disabled, reinforcing other social disadvantages.

A further consequence could be the creation of a third underclass, namely those who are unemployed for lengthy periods. Not only will this group find it harder to obtain "good" jobs, but they can also find themselves moving in and out of the work force on a regular basis, undergoing the trauma and stresses associated with losing a job on each occasion.

Another important factor leading to the loss of jobs involves company takeovers and mergers that lead to the creation of large, multinational conglomerates. Jobs invariably are lost when two large companies merge because of the elimination of duplicated services or processes, the closure of less profitable or desirable parts of the new operation, and/or the moving of the corporate headquarters of one of the companies involved.

In the summer of 1986, for example, in San Francisco alone eight companies were involved in mergers or takeovers, with a projected loss of 13,000 jobs within the surrounding area (Table 2–1) (San Francisco Chronicle 1986). The major reasons for the job losses were the closure of the head offices of one of the companies involved and the relocation of manufacturing processes to other parts of the country where production costs were lower.

Over the last three years there has been an increase in the number of hostile takeovers and leveraged buyouts, both of which can be very damaging to a company's financial well-being. In these situations a company or a group of investors will attempt to purchase a controlling share of another company that does not wish to sell by buying its stock, often with money borrowed against the assets of the target company. If the takeover is successful, assets of the company will be sold or realized and less profitable parts of the new operation closed to raise capital to repay the loan. However, to resist a hostile takeover a company may have to spend many millions of dollars to buy its own stock, often creating cash flow problems that necessitate cutbacks or layoffs. Either way, the target company is significantly affected, its productivity can be reduced, and the amount of capital available for maintaining or expanding production, and hence the work force, is diminished. The new investors may have little commitment to or understanding of the company they are pursuing, and in a few days they can overturn many years of effort by the company's work force or shareholders.

Another major threat to jobs comes from the consolida-

TABLE 2–1. Projected job losses in San Francisco due to company mergers or takeovers in 1986

Company	Taken over by	Jobs lost	Reason
Crocker National	Wells Fargo	5,000	Duplication
Southern Pacific Transportation Co.	Santa Fe Railway	1,000	Moving headquarters
Crown Zellerbach	James River Co.; James Goldsmith	350	Moving headquarters
Pacific Telephone	Internal reorganization	5,000	Lower real estate costs
Del Monte	R.J.R. Nabisco	1,000	Consolidation of work force
Castle & Cooke	David Murdock	185	Moving headquarters
Itel Corp.	Samuel Zell	35	Moving company

Source. Adapted from San Francisco Chronicle 1986.

tion of large multinational corporations that view their activities at a global level. With this kind of perspective, less profitable parts of an organization can be closed on a whim by executives who have no allegiance to a community even though it may depend heavily on the jobs being eliminated. Computerization in the banking and commercial worlds has also made it easier to move capital from one country to another.

Branch plants of large corporations are particularly vulnerable. Corporations that are overextended or that wish to consolidate may close smaller parts of their operation, especially if they have unrealistically high expectations of yield or productivity. A company will be much less inclined to close down a company headquarters or "flagship" plant that may have been the first step in the organization's development, but may have little loyalty to a smaller, more distant community.

Another result of the global approach taken by larger corporations has been the shifting of production to less-developed countries where labor costs are reduced and profits are accordingly higher. An example of this has been the establishment of the Maquiladora Zone in Northern Mexico. It runs along the entire length of the border with the United States and now contains over 1,600 factories with 420,000 employees. Wages are approximately a tenth of American rates, and if raw materials are imported from the United States the finished product can be reimported without having to pay duty on anything but the costs of labor. Many American and Canadian companies have relocated in Mexico to increase their profitability, leaving the work force in the original communities without jobs. These kinds of actions can also be employed as a strategy to reduce the power of organized labor or disrupt collective bargaining processes.

In addition, many small, isolated communities often depend upon a single industry, which is often based upon the development of a natural resource. When the resource becomes depleted or a cheaper or more profitable alternative can be developed elsewhere, the industry may be closed. The consequences can be traumatic. Secondary industries, such as small businesses and services that depend directly or indirectly on revenues from the employer, may face bankruptcy, and the town can lose a significant portion of its tax base. For these communities, economic diversification is often not possible because of limited local markets and high transportation costs.

Workers laid off in these situations have limited work alternatives. Younger workers may feel impelled to move away from the community—and their roots—to find work elsewhere, but may be ill-prepared to make the adjustment to a larger community or unable to afford the higher costs of accommodation. The departure of young people, leaving behind a preponderance of older, married people, changes the demographic balance of the community. Older workers faced with the same situation may have to accept demeaning or poorly paid jobs, take early retirement, or move to a new community.

Workers who are forced to relocate often face multiple obstacles. They may have limited resources and few supports in the communities to which they move, with little first-hand knowledge of their new environment and ways of finding work. These workers may be adjusting to life in a large town for the first time, while slowly realizing that the skills they possess may not be required or are irrelevant in a large urban context.

Farming communities are also faced with major upheavals or dislocations. In addition to economic factors, farmers also have to contend with climatic forces such as drought or crop failure that may imperil their livelihood. Many farmers who chose to expand during more prosperous times in the 1970s found themselves with excessive debt loads when the economy worsened and interest rates rose. Some have had to take a second job to maintain their farm, and others have been forced from the land permanently. In Saskatchewan alone, an agricultural province in the Canadian prairies with a population of less than a million, 17,000 farms closed between May 1987 and May 1988 (Sunday Star 1988).

One other economic factor that may lead to the loss of jobs is an increase in "free trade" agreements that remove tariffs or barriers to imports. It is likely that agreements such as that signed in 1989 between Canada and the United States, and the elimination of trade barriers within the European Economic Community in 1992, will lead to the closure of specific local industries that are unable to compete and to an increase in regional disparity and economic hardship for communities that may already be disadvantaged. For example, Philips—a large electronics corporation—is now predicting that it will close 120 of its 200 European plants after trade barriers are removed in 1992.

Changing Role of Women

The third major factor that is changing the composition of the work force is the increased participation of women (Fuchs

1983). More than 50% of North American women now work (Townson 1986). There are an increasing number of two-income and single-parent families, and the "traditional" family structure in which the father works and the mother stays home to care for the children now applies to fewer than one in seven of all households (Task Force on Child Care 1986).

The pattern of female participation in the work force has also changed. In previous years women would have been more likely to have worked until their childbearing years but then would not have returned to work until their children were grown up. Today many more mothers return to work while their children are still of preschool age. In 1985, 54% of all Canadian women with children under the age of 3 were working, two-thirds of them full-time (Statistics Canada 1985). Not only is this quicker return to work changing the composition of the work force, but it is also challenging families to look at styles of parenting and adjust to the stress created by the conflict between work demands and family life.

Despite these changes, women's work is still sectorized, with 75% of all women's jobs being in the traditional areas of clerical work, nursing, service, teaching, and sales (Conelly 1978). And while the increased income can produce greater independence and autonomy for married women, an increasing number of working women are single parents who face additional obstacles to their participation in the work force. In 1988 the average annual family wage in Canada was $48,000 for two-parent families but only $18,000 for one-parent families (Hamilton Spectator 1988). This latter group includes a disproportionately high percentage of the working poor, who frequently have no option but to accept "bad" jobs with lower pay and little long-term security.

The Aging Population

The demographic balance of the population is changing as people are living longer and are capable of working to a later age. And as members of the "baby boom" generation grow older, the work force will include an increasing percentage of individuals who are over 45 years of age.

This increase in the number of older workers could have many repercussions. If more older workers stay in their jobs, there will be fewer opportunities for advancement and promotion and a smaller number of job vacancies, making it harder for younger people to break into the work force.

One possible but controversial solution is early retirement (Ross 1985; Gordus 1980). While this could ease the employment problems of some younger workers, it could lead to increasing numbers of healthy older people being denied the opportunity to work. It may also create differentials between blue-collar workers, who may have no choice in whether to retire, and professionals, who may have the option of working on.

There is also evidence that older workers have a harder time coping with the impact of unemployment. They may have to overcome biases on the part of prospective employers and a lack of jobs for which they are qualified, as well as possibly experiencing additional physical problems, all of which may lead to them remaining unemployed for lengthy periods of time.

Each of these factors is likely to increase the number of people facing a period of unemployment over the next decade, although it is impossible to estimate accurately as to how many. Before looking at how these people can best be helped, we need to review what we already know about how unemployment can affect individuals, families, and communities.

References

Ayres R, Miller S: The Impact of Robotics on the Workforce and Workplace. Pittsburgh, PA, Robotics Institute, Carnegie-Mellon University, 1981

Bergmann F: The Freedom of New Work. Toronto, Canadian Mental Health Association, 1986

Best F: Work Sharing: Issues, Policy Options and Prospects.

Kalamazoo, MI, WE Upjohn Institute for Employment Research, 1981

Conelly P: Last Hired First Fired: Women and the Canadian Work Force. Toronto, Women's Press, 1978

Fuchs VR: How We Live: An Economic Perspective on Americans from Birth to Death. Cambridge, MA, Harvard University Press, 1983

Gordus JP: Leaving Early: Perspectives and Problems in Current Retirement Practice and Policy. Kalamazoo, MI, WE Upjohn Institute for Employment Research, 1980

Hamilton Spectator, Nov 8, 1988, A8

Handy C: The Future of Work. Oxford, UK, Blackwell, 1985

Howland M: Plant Closings and Worker Displacement: The Regional Issues. Kalamazoo, MI, WE Upjohn Institute for Employment Research, 1988

Hunt HA, Hunt TL: Human Resources: Implications of Robotics. Kalamazoo, MI, WE Upjohn Institute for Employment Research, 1983

Hunt HA, Hunt TL: Clerical Employment and Technological Change. Kalamazoo, MI, WE Upjohn Institute for Employment Research, 1986

Levitan S, Johnson C: Second Thoughts on Work. Kalamazoo, MI, WE Upjohn Institute for Employment Research, 1982

New Orleans Times Picayune, Oct 27, 1988, A1

Novick M: Work and Well-Being: Social Choices of a Healthy Society. Toronto, Canadian Mental Health Association, 1986

People's Commission on Unemployment in Newfoundland and Labrador: Now That We've Burnt Our Boats. St. John's, Newfoundland, Newfoundland and Labrador Federation of Labour, 1978

Pierson F: The Minimum Level of Unemployment and Public Policy. Kalamazoo, MI, WE Upjohn Institute for Employment Research, 1980

Reid F: Public Policies for Alternative Work Arrangements. Toronto, Canadian Mental Health Association, 1986

Robertson J: Future Work. Aldershot, Hampshire, UK, Gower Publishing, 1985

Ross M (ed): The Economics of Aging. Kalamazoo, MI, WE Upjohn Institute for Employment Research, 1985

San Francisco Chronicle, May 27, 1986, Part 4, p 8

Smith R: More evidence on unemployment and health (editorial). Br Med J 294:1047–1048, 1987

Statistics Canada: Unemployment rates—Canada (table). Labour Force Information 39(12):7, 1983

Statistics Canada: Estimates of female heads (or spouse) of family by labour force status and family composition (table). The Labour Force 41(12):36, 1985

Statistics Canada: Employment rates by province—January 1989 (table). The Labour Force 45(1):B2, 1989

Sunday Star (Toronto), July 24, 1988, B1

Task Force on Child Care, Canadian Committee for the Status of Women: Status of Women. Toronto, Canadian Committee for the Status of Women, 1986

Therborn G: Why Some People Are More Unemployed Than Others. London, Verso, 1986

Toronto Globe and Mail, Oct 8, 1988

Townson M: A New Work Agenda for Women. Toronto, Canadian Mental Health Association, 1986

U.S. Department of Labor, Bureau of Labor Statistics: Annual data: employment status of the civilian working-age population, approximating U.S. concepts, 10 countries (table). Monthly Labor Rev 111(12):101, 1988

Zuboff S: In the Age of the Smart Machine: The Future of Work and Power. New York, Basic Books, 1988

Chapter 3

Impact of Job Loss: What We Know

Chapter 3

Impact of Job Loss: What We Know

> We entered Marienthal as scientists—we leave it with only one desire: that the tragic opportunity for such an inquiry may not recur in our time.
> Researcher working with Marie Jahoda in Marienthal

While much has been written on the psychosocial impact of job loss, the psychiatric literature contains relatively few scientifically sound studies. Moreover, much of the research that has taken place has been carried out in single communities where specific local factors have had a bearing on the outcome. Consequently, these findings cannot necessarily be directly transposed from one community to another.

Researchers have focused on diverse aspects of the relationship between unemployment and mental health. Some have reviewed changes in national data, some have followed groups of unemployed workers and described what happens to them, and some have taken particular characteristics of workers or workplaces and examined their relationship to job loss. Not surprisingly, the variation in research methodologies and approaches has led to some conflicting findings.

When examining these studies, therefore, it is necessary to look at each one as providing a piece of a large puzzle. Not only are there many findings that are consistent from study to study, but even seemingly contradictory conclusions may prove to be complementary if allowance is made for the limitations of the methodology. Our aim in reviewing these studies is to integrate their findings to provide a framework for clinical interventions.

Types of Studies

Previous studies of the impact of unemployment can be categorized under four broad headings: descriptive; macro level; cross-sectional micro level; longitudinal micro level. Many of the descriptive studies were conducted in times of earlier economic recessions, particularly during the 1930s. Even today, our lack of understanding of the impact of unemployment highlights the need for thoughtful descriptive studies that raise questions and pave the way for further research.

Macro level studies correlate fluctuations in indicators of economic activity, such as unemployment rates, with changes in the incidence or prevalence of health, mental health, and social problems, and the utilization of services at a national, regional, or local level.

Micro level studies examine relevant characteristics of individuals or of smaller, clearly defined populations. Longitudinal studies identify a cohort and follow its progress. This cohort may be drawn from a single workplace or may represent a group of unemployed individuals who are defined by other criteria such as living in the same community or utilizing a specific service. Cross-sectional studies have usually taken one of two routes. In the first, a group of unemployed workers are surveyed at a specific point in time to examine factors that may have contributed to their current problems. In the second, a random population sample is surveyed to identify differences between those who are working and those who are not.

These studies have been conducted in three broad chronological periods. The first was the 1930s, during which time many moving descriptions of the impact of the Depression on unemployed workers and their families were produced (Jahoda et al. 1971; Bakke 1940; Pilgrim Trust 1938; Marsh 1938; Eisenberg and Lazarsfeld 1938; Komarovsky 1940). Unemployment levels receded both during and after World War II, and little further was written on unemployment until the late 1950s, when the postwar boom slowed down and the effects of economic change began to be felt.

During the 1960s and the early 1970s, which were still years of relatively low unemployment, studies focused primarily on the closing of single plants and the impact on workers who were displaced. These studies concentrated less on mental health problems and more on difficulties in reentering the work force as a measurement of outcome.

This period also produced some important macro level studies that linked unemployment and other indicators of economic activity to a variety of health and mental health outcomes. The most influential of these came from M. Harvey Brenner (1973), who gave credibility to the concept of a link between unemployment and mental health problems, and who helped to draw the attention of national policymakers to the plight of the unemployed.

The third collection of studies has been stimulated by the sudden rise in unemployment at the beginning of the 1980s. It is no coincidence that many of these studies originated in Great Britain, which felt the impact of higher levels of unemployment earlier and to a more severe degree than either Canada or the United States. These studies have taken a more sophisticated approach to study design and data analysis. In addition to conducting outcome studies, researchers have attempted to identify the components in the complex chain of events that progress from job loss to emotional distress, to analyze the role of important intervening variables such as social support or work attitudes, and to identify groups at risk. Prospective researchers, however, face many methodological obstacles.

Most research has concentrated on plant closures, because they provide the most likely source of a cohort to study. However, this is only one way in which workers can lose their jobs. Partial layoffs or the firing of individuals or small groups of workers receives much less attention. The course of these workers' problems may be very different, and workers coping with these problems are much harder to identify and follow as a group.

The analysis of macro level data poses different problems.

The evidence is often inferential, and the inclusion criteria or definition of a problem being analyzed is often unclear and may vary from place to place. For example, the rate of hospitalization—a commonly used indicator—can depend on bed availability, the number of psychiatrists in a community, financial cutbacks, philosophies of treatment, and the availability of alternative community services. Many indicators represent only those cases who are identified or who choose to seek help, and so do not accurately reflect either the incidence or the prevalence of a problem. Moreover, because these indicators measure aggregate data, it is likely that variations in overall rates will not reflect changes in small sections of the population or those caused by other factors (such as socioeconomic class) that are not taken into consideration.

Methodological Difficulties

The difficulties in mounting a study at the workplace or community (micro) level can be formidable. The first challenge comes when trying to assemble a large enough cohort to study. Many workers may not be willing to participate, and those who are interested may find new employment before the study begins. There is often only a brief time period to organize a project before layoffs begin, and accurate preunemployment profiles cannot always be obtained.

Even if a cohort can be assembled, it may not be a random or representative sample of workers from that particular workplace or community, and a single workplace is rarely typical of the work force in general. Many studies have taken place at unionized plants, because these plants usually provide easier access to the work force, and have concentrated on male-dominated plants or industries that may have had a relatively stable work force. As a result, findings in any one workplace can provide broad pointers but cannot always be extrapolated directly to other work situations.

Assembling a control group can also create difficulties, especially if an entire plant is closing and controls have to be found from other workplaces. In addition to demographic factors (i.e., age, sex, race, marital status), numerous other variables, such as level of education, commitment to the workplace, financial well-being, or personality factors, have all been shown to affect the outcome, but it can be hard to cross-match for these variables when setting up a control group.

Findings

The literature dealing with the relationship between job loss and mental health provides findings that, at first glance, appear contradictory. For example, Brenner (1973) has argued that unemployment itself causes increases in mental health problems and psychopathology, whereas Catalano et al. (1985) suggest that unemployment may uncover, rather than create, social and psychiatric pathology. Aiken et al. (1969), in their study of Packard Motor Company workers who had been laid off from one plant, found economic deprivation to be the most significant factor affecting long-term outcome. By contrast, Cobb and Kasl (1977), in another much-quoted study, found little evidence to support this finding. Some authors have identified loss and grieving as the major mechanism that leads to emotional distress (Strange 1978; Borgen and Amundsen 1984; Warr 1985), while others have felt that the stress involved in unemployment is the most important factor (Jacobsen 1987; Baum et al. 1985).

Some of these differences stem from the way studies are designed. Longitudinal studies that do not have the benefit of accurate preunemployment data may be more likely to view job loss as a causative event and interpret outcome data in this light. On the other hand, cross-sectional studies may assess preunemployment factors more closely and be more inclined to conclude that unemployment exposes preexisting problems.

The fact that different approaches and mechanisms have been postulated does not necessarily mean that some are correct or that certain findings should be disregarded. What is more likely is that each approach is addressing a part of the overall problem. Moreover, despite the differences among ap-proaches, there are many recurring themes and common find-ings, such as greater difficulties faced by older workers in finding new jobs, changes in self-esteem of those workers who lose their jobs, and the impact of unemployment on the fam-ilies of the jobless.

Viewing these studies collectively, rather than in isolation, allows two conclusions to be drawn. The first is the importance of taking a multifactorial approach to understanding the ways in which losing a job may affect a person. The second is that the differing approaches are not exclusive but may in fact be complementary. The key to successful interventions with indi-vidual cases is knowing which mechanisms or models are the most applicable in a specific situation.

Macro Level Studies

At various times fluctuations in employment rates have been linked to changes in the incidence of alcoholism (Smart 1979; Winton et al. 1986; Iversen and Klausen 1986; Crawford et al. 1985; Office of Population Censuses and Surveys 1984), spouse and child abuse (Nichols 1976; Justice and Duncan 1977; Krugman et al. 1986; Creighton 1984; Taitz et al. 1987), family breakdown (Popay 1984; Fagin and Little 1984), van-dalism and criminal behavior (Borus 1984; Gillespie 1975), psychiatric hospitalizations (Ahr et al. 1981; Catalano et al. 1981), suicide (Platt 1986; Platt and Duffy 1986; Platt and Kreitman 1985; Hawton and Rose 1986; Boor 1980; Lester 1970), homicide (Brenner 1973), and a variety of physical complaints and illnesses (Moser et al. 1986; Smith 1985a; Linn et al. 1985; Hagen 1983; Group for the Advancement of Psy-chiatry 1982; Colledge and Hainsworth 1982; Bunn 1979; Fisher 1965; Thurlow 1971).

A seminal contribution to the macro level approach came from the work of Brenner in the early 1970s (Brenner 1973, 1979). He reviewed changes in different indicators of eco-nomic activity that had shown cyclical variations over 127 years, and then correlated these changes with the rates for seven specific indicators—cardiac disease, liver disease, suicide, homicide, psychiatric hospitalizations, alcoholism, and overall mortality. Brenner demonstrated that changes in economic activity could lead to a specific number of new cases for each of these indicators. He suggested that in the United States, a 1.5% rise in unemployment in 1 year could be responsible for an additional 51,570 deaths and 5,520 hospitalizations over the following 5 years. He also identified a lag period between the increase in unemployment and changes in an indicator of 1 year for suicide and homicide and as long as 3 years for cardiovascular disease.

Brenner's findings, replicated in a study of mortality rates in the United Kingdom over a 40-year period (Brenner 1979), are complex and have to some extent been challenged by other authors (see Eyer 1977; Grayson 1985). For example, the lag of 2–3 years after peaks in unemployment levels is not consistent with the findings of many studies of single plant closures. These studies have demonstrated that mental health problems can be recognized within weeks of the layoff and in some instances even before it takes place.

In addition, although losing a job may be a single event, it takes place within a particular social context (e.g., inadequate social support or limited work alternatives) that may be making the major contribution to a person's problems and whose effects can be intensified during any period of economic deprivation. Unemployment can also bring in its wake other personal setbacks such as migration or family breakdown that may be even more stressful than the loss of the job. The approaches used by Brenner and others did not allow for the numerous variables that can contribute to the loss of a job and affect the outcome of this event. It is fair to say, however, that Brenner's work helped to refocus attention on the link between unemployment and mental health problems and its implication for social policy.

Eyer (1977) has also studied the impact of changes in a variety of business cycles on social indicators but reached different conclusions from Brenner. Eyer believes that periods of economic growth could also be disruptive and that social stress and community fragmentation peak at the height of the business cycle. These factors would then contribute to the development of physical and emotional problems, whose presence would appear to coincide with downturns in the economy or increases in unemployment rates. Eyer sees unemployment itself as contributing only a small percentage of the increase in death rates.

While there is general agreement, therefore, that unemployment is associated with emotional distress, there is not a consensus as to the extent to which this distress may be caused by the creation of new difficulties, by the exacerbation of preexisting problems, or by a deterioration in social conditions that are already stressful.

This question was addressed by Catalano et al. (1985). While not discounting the role of unemployment in "provoking" mental health problems, these authors believe unemployment could also create social conditions that would lead to individuals with preexisting problems having their deficits "uncovered."

To demonstrate this effect the authors studied data from the Monroe County case register in New York State. They examined the association between manufacturing employment rates and first admissions to a state psychiatric hospital in order to test three hypotheses: manufacturing employment was inversely related to first admissions of individuals who (a) might have had previous psychiatric treatment, (b) had definitely had previous psychiatric treatment, and (c) had had no previous psychiatric treatment.

Catalano et al. analyzed these data using the "transfer-function modeling" method of Box and Jenkins (1976) and concluded that there was an association between employment rates and people who might have had a previous admission. These authors found no evidence of a relationship between unemployment and first state-hospital admissions for individuals without a previous psychiatric contact. This finding suggested that unemployment was not creating new problems. There was, however, a strong association between employment rates and individuals who had had a previous psychiatric contact, especially for men. These findings support the role of unemployment in uncovering psychiatric problems.

Catalano et al. also found that the lag period between economic change and the presentation of symptoms was approximately 3 months. This figure is less than the time frame proposed by Brenner but more in keeping with expected clinical outcomes in response to a life crisis as well as with the findings of research on single plant closures. These authors also found that women appeared to respond more rapidly to economic change than did men, as evidenced by the time between rises in unemployment rates and increases in hospital admission rates. This difference in response rate may reflect previously identified sex differences in patterns of seeking help.

The authors concluded by stressing the importance of distinguishing change in the total variance in service utilization rates caused by all predictive factors from change in explained variance due to the contribution of unemployment alone. They felt that in Monroe County, after other variables had been removed, changes in manufacturing employment rates added only 7% to the overall variance in hospitalization rates. These authors also highlighted the importance of separating social significance from statistical significance, the former being a term that depends on political rather than empirical analysis.

Micro Level Studies—Cross-Sectional Studies

Two problems complicate cross-sectional studies. The first is that inferences have to be made as to the direction of the relationship between preunemployment variables and postunemployment outcomes when looking at a population sample at a single point in time. The second is assembling a large enough cohort to obtain a representative sample that will allow for all of the variables that need to be taken into account. Despite these problems, cross-sectional studies have added to the evidence supporting a link between unemployment and mental health problems, and have identified areas for further investigation.

D'Arcy (1986) reviewed data from the 1981 Canada Health Study, which collected information on 32,000 individuals in 12,000 households across Canada. Health status measures utilized included an affective balance scale for psychological distress, 16 items derived from the health opinion survey for anxiety and depressive symptoms, and the number of disability days.

One-way analysis of variance showed that the unemployed experienced significantly more general psychological distress, anxiety and depressive symptoms, disability days, activity limitation, and health problems, and made more hospital visits and telephone calls to physicians than did those who were employed. When regression analysis was carried out, it was found that the unemployed experienced more ill-health than did the employed. Unemployed individuals under 40 reported greater psychological distress and more anxiety and depressive symptoms, while older unemployed workers reported more physician visits.

Socioeconomic status generally exerted a substantial effect on the unemployment-health relationship, with unemployed people having low incomes reporting greater psychological distress and more anxiety and depressive symptoms. The unemployed individuals who were principal family wage earners reported the most psychological distress. Data on the effects of other potentially moderating factors such as work commitment, personal aspirations, and recreational activities, were not available. One of D'Arcy's conclusions from these data was that the negative effects of unemployment reflect wider social inequities.

This issue was examined more closely by Arber (1987), who reviewed data from a similar survey in the United Kingdom—the 1981–1982 General Household Survey. She analyzed data on socioeconomic class, employment status, and the presence of limiting physical illness in a sample of approximately 28,000 men and women chosen at random. The study used a socioeconomic classification of occupational class consisting of six categories ranging from unskilled to professional.

Arber found that the unskilled group had twice as much limiting long-standing illness as the professional group and that there were higher mortality rates for both men and women in the lower socioeconomic classes. There was a standardized mortality rate (SMR; mean = 100) of 66 for the highest class and 165 for the lowest class. She also found the unemployment rate to be seven times higher for unskilled men when compared to professionals. This finding suggests that while low socioeconomic class and unemployment are both independently associated with poor health, there is a considerable amount of overlap. Membership in a lower socioeconomic class increased the likelihood of losing a job and contributed to a greater degree of distress when a job was lost.

There was a weaker relationship between class position and health outcomes for women than there was for men, possibly because the socioeconomic class of married women was defined by their husbands' occupation. This difference could also be explained by the preparedness of many women, especially second wage earners, to take on jobs that were not equivalent to their husbands' occupational status if there was less pressure to bring in a supporting wage.

Micro Level Studies—Longitudinal Studies

Many studies of the aftereffects of plant closure carried out in North America in the 1960s and 1970s focused on success in finding new work as the major outcome criterion. One of the first groups to examine the link between plant closure and mental health was Aiken et al. (1969), who conducted a study of employees laid off by the Packard Motor Company. To measure emotional well-being—or its absence—a five-item morale scale based on workers' attitudes was used. The major finding of this study was that workers with economic security (e.g., those who possessed financial resources or marketable skills), as measured by an economic deprivation scale, had higher scores on the morale scale than those who did not have economic security. This finding highlighted the possible importance of economic deprivation on the well-being of unemployed workers' mental health. However, the study failed to demonstrate a direct link between unemployment and economic deprivation or to indicate whether those workers with additional resources also had other personal strengths that helped them withstand the stress they faced. Unlike the index of economic deprivation, previous labor market experiences were found to have little or no predictive value in relation to mental health.

The authors came to three conclusions. First, certain factors that existed prior to the loss of the job could predict labor market outcomes. (For example, older workers might experience longer periods of unemployment.) Second, labor market outcomes such as success in finding new work were related to less economic deprivation. Finally, economic deprivation and other stressors accompanying unemployment were the link between losing a job, behavioral and attitudinal problems, and labor market outcomes. In these authors' opinion the availability of economic resources is the single most important factor affecting the morale and mental health of the jobless worker.

One of the most influential studies from the early 1970s was carried out by Cobb and Kasl (1977). This study was a comprehensive and well-designed attempt to assess the impact of job loss on workers in two unnamed plants that closed in 1969. One plant was a paint manufacturing factory located in an urban area; the other was a heavy industrial enterprise located in a rural area. The target group was 100 married, male blue-collar workers aged 35–60 who had worked at the plants for more than 3 years. The controls were drawn from four workplaces that performed similar work and maintained the rural-urban balance. Eighty percent of selected workers participated.

Workers were assessed at four points in time over 2 years,

the first assessment coming 6 weeks prior to the closing of the plant. A number of instruments and scales were utilized to assess various health and social outcomes or to provide validity checks. The major emphasis in analysis and interpretation was placed on two indices—relative economic deprivation and relative economic change—both adopted from the Packard study. Physical indicators of stress, such as changes in blood uric acid and cholesterol levels and in blood pressure, were also included.

Cobb and Kasl found that the unemployment experiences differed in rural and urban workers. The average period of unemployment for the study was 15 weeks. In the urban setting 25% of workers found work immediately and 50% were unemployed for less than 2 months, whereas workers in the rural setting experienced more difficulty in finding new jobs. The situation improved for rural workers over the course of the study, especially as they were less likely to experience a further period of unemployment. By the end of the second year the period of time spent out of work was the same for each group, but urban workers were more likely to have experienced further episodes of unemployment and greater disruption in their lives.

Cobb and Kasl did not find any consistently high level of distress among unemployed workers, although the period of apprehension prior to the plant closing was the time of greatest anxiety and depression. This period was also the time of greatest increase in the physical indicators of stress. The authors believe that most workers adapted to unemployment over time, with those who experienced further episodes faring the worst, although for some workers the emotional changes continued after new work was found.

These findings led Cobb and Kasl to state explicitly that "the mental health aspect of job loss and unemployment appears to be a limited one, both in terms of magnitude as well as in terms of duration." Other authors who have studied longer-term outcomes of plant closures, often using methodologies or analyses similar to those used by Cobb and Kasl, have come

45

up with different findings. Part of the reason for this discrepancy may be that Cobb and Kasl's target population may have had a relatively weak investment in their work, or had begun to detach themselves from their workplace months or even years before the plant closed. These workers were also laid off at a time when further work was relatively easy to find. The average length of an episode of unemployment (15 weeks) was just over half of the average length of a period of unemployment in 1983 (27 weeks) (Statistics Canada 1983).

More recently, Grayson (1985) employed a similar methodology to study the impact of the closure of a ball-bearing manufacturing factory in Toronto. Employees and their spouses were surveyed 5 months prior to termination, at termination, and at 7 weeks, 6 months, and 1 and 2 years after termination. These periods were chosen to correspond with Cobb and Kasl's time frame. Grayson created an index of distress based on three questions: how much the shutdown bothered the worker, how long before things got back to normal, and the ranking of the stress generated by the closure as a life event.

In this study, the stress attributed to the closure by the unemployed workers changed very little over time and was consistently higher for those individuals who remained unemployed. When the impact of unemployment on workers' spouses was examined, the level of stress was significantly higher at 6 months after termination than at termination. At the end of 2 years the amount of stress experienced by both the unemployed workers and their spouses remained high, in contrast to the findings of Cobb and Kasl.

Cobb and Kasl had also found that ill-health, as measured by a questionnaire and analysis of stress-related physical indicators, had peaked at the time of termination and then decreased. In order to further examine this course, Grayson collected additional data on three other health indicators: the number of physician visits, the use of prescribed medication, and the evaluation of health determinants. When the results were viewed collectively Grayson found that the unemployed had had more health problems than the employed prior to the closure and that unemployment appears to have contributed to a continuation of these problems. He also found that the health of the unemployed worker worsened during the period following the closure, although not significantly.

Grayson then conducted a path analysis of the variables involved and arrived at the following conclusions: (a) There was a direct link between stress attributed to the shutdown and the onset of family problems; (b) The greater an individual's social activity, the lower the level of stress experienced; (c) There was a link between economic deprivation and stress for spouses of jobless workers; (d) Economic deprivation was not the most important factor in determining health and mental health outcomes of unemployment.

Grayson also stated that the impact of unemployment on health and the stress it generated were immediate, contrary to the concept of the 2- or 3-year lag period suggested by Brenner (see above). As the period of unemployment lengthened, the direct relationship between the stress of losing the job and ill health appeared to dissipate. Unemployed individuals continued to experience high levels of stress and problems with their health, but factors other than unemployment contributed to this to an increasing degree.

Examining a wider range of workplaces, Atkinson et al. (1986) studied 40 blue-collar and 40 white-collar male workers and their families drawn from different workplaces after the involuntary loss of their jobs in the Boston area. Each of the unemployed workers' families was matched with a control for characteristics such as occupation, work status of wife, life cycle status, and locality. All families had at least one child under the age of 18 living with them. Four extensive interviews were conducted over a 1-year period.

This study resulted in two major findings. First, unemployed men showed higher levels of psychiatric symptomatology at 1 to 4 months after losing their job when compared with the control group. The greatest difference was found at 4 months. Those workers who returned to work during the study

47

period showed decreased stress levels to a point that was lower than those of the controls, possibly due to a compensatory effect upon becoming reemployed. Second, the wives of the unemployed workers were significantly more depressed, anxious, phobic, and sensitive about their interpersonal relationships than control spouses at 4 months. In contrast, the levels of psychiatric symptomatology in the wives of reemployed workers were indistinguishable from those of the wives of controls at this time.

Atkinson et al. hypothesized that the stress experienced by the husbands due to their jobless state was transmitted to the family system. Wives did not experience the personal loss of the job directly, but they were exposed to changes in family relationships as the mood and behavior of their unemployed partner changed. Over time the husbands' role performance changed and their supportiveness decreased, leading to changes in the wives' role performance. Measures of family cohesion, organization, and conflict also indicated that unemployed families became significantly more stressed than controls by the fourth month of unemployment. The authors perceived the outcome of the reemployed group to be essential to their analysis, and they inferred from the selective experience of this group that unemployment is a cause of—rather than a response to—emotional strain, which diminishes rapidly when a new job is found.

Unemployment and Social Support

There is increasing evidence that social support can reduce the impact of stress, social isolation, or personal reversal. Social support is not, however, a unitary concept; it has many different facets, including financial assistance, companionship, advice, joint activities, and a sense of personal continuity. The importance of each of these factors varies according to the needs of the individual or the demands of the situation.

Recent studies have raised two important issues that have broadened the understanding of a social support system. The first has been the need to define the role and value of social support, assessing whether it increases an individual's ability to cope or serves to buffer the effects of environmental stress. The second has been to define the particular characteristics or functions of a social support network that are most helpful in times of unemployment.

Gore (1978) reviewed data from the Cobb and Kasl study to examine these issues. Measures of stress utilized included the number of weeks of unemployment and the degree of economic deprivation. Dependent health variables included scales to measure depression and self-blame, illness symptoms, and serum cholesterol levels. Social support was measured by a 13-item scale covering perceptions of support, frequency of activities outside the home, and perception of opportunities to participate in activities. Perceived economic deprivation was derived from two items that covered income in comparison with neighbors and difficulties in coping.

Gore found that social support did not affect the impact of economic deprivation itself, but did buffer perceptions of economic deprivation. This finding indicated that the perception of economic deprivation should be seen as an important additional response to unemployment. The amount of social support did not correlate with measures of illness behavior and physiological change. The author also examined reasons why workers in rural communities might have experienced less disruption than urban workers, and hypothesized that the rural communities had a greater cohesion and kinship and responded more energetically to threats to their economic base than did the urban communities.

In summary, Gore sees supportive relationships as helping to maintain a sense of self-worth for those unemployed workers who are unable to make instrumental accomplishments in social activities. The absence of these relationships would lead to a lowering of self-esteem and a greater likelihood of emotional difficulties.

Ullah et al. (1985) examined some of the components that make up a support network. They studied 1,150 unemployed

17-year-olds with low levels of education, living in 11 urban regions in England. The authors focused on two particular groups of respondents: (a) those who had few social contacts, and (b) those whose social contacts included a high proportion of other unemployed individuals.

Affective well-being or distress was assessed using scales that measured the presence of minor psychiatric morbidity, depression, anxiety, concern over unemployment, and perceptions of the stigma of being unemployed. Social supports were measured by a five-item social support scale, the number of contacts with other unemployed people, and the number of peer contacts. Moderating variables were employment commitment and perceived pressure to obtain a job.

Although the social support inter-item correlations were moderately high, scores for individual items showed differences. The two forms of support with the strongest association with well-being were financial assistance and suggestions for interesting things to do—both instrumental support functions. Decreased peer group contact was moderately associated with increased depression and concern over unemployment. Greater contact with other unemployed people led to less concern about unemployment and its stigma. Perceived pressure to obtain a job was directly related to all measures of distress, and the greater the pressure the greater the distress. Thus the experience of unemployment may lead to the establishment of new, unsupportive relationships or to a perceived lack of support from those to whom a young person might turn for help.

The authors also found that certain kinds of support were more beneficial for certain sex and ethnic subgroups. Females lacking someone to cheer them up were more likely to have higher distress scores than males, while whites were more likely to benefit from having someone to suggest things to do than were blacks. The authors concluded that their study provides partial support for the theory of stress-buffering, although certain supports only buffered certain kinds of stresses. They emphasized the need for further research to look at causal relationships and to investigate the role of social support systems before, as well as after, a period of unemployment is experienced.

Outcomes of Unemployment

Physical Health

Changes in physical health have been documented by both the presence of illness or symptoms and an increased utilization of health services. Many of the reported short-term changes in physical health, often measured by screening instruments such as the Generalized Health Questionnaire (GHQ) or by changes in physical indicators such as increases in blood pressure or serum cholesterol levels, are similar to those experienced by individuals at times of stress or crisis.

Longer-term health problems are harder to demonstrate because of the possibility of undetected or quiescent problems that are exacerbated or exposed by unemployment. One frequent long-term effect of unemployment, reported by a number of authors, is an increase in the likelihood of developing cardiovascular problems (Moser et al. 1986; Brenner 1973, 1987; Bunn 1979). Brenner (1973) originally suggested that a 1% increase in unemployment could lead to a 2% increase in cardiovascular mortality rates over a 3-year period. In a further study he reviewed the correlation between cardiovascular disease mortality rates and unemployment rates in nine industrialized countries between 1954 and 1978. Using a multivariate analysis he was able to control for the effects of smoking and animal fat consumption, both of which increase the risk of heart disease (Brenner 1987). The author found a positive association between unemployment and increased heart disease mortality in all nine countries. Cardiovascular disease is one area in which the concept of a 2- to 3-year lag period fits clinical evidence, because it may take a number of years for stress-induced effects to lead to pathological changes.

One other study of importance in this area is the longitudinal study by the Office of Population Censuses and Surveys in the United Kingdom, which compared mortality patterns of 6,000 unemployed workers aged 15–64 with a larger sample of employed individuals, drawn from the general population, over a 10-year period, beginning in 1971 (Moser et al. 1986). Unemployed males had a higher overall mortality rate, with a standardized mortality rate (SMR) of 137, compared to the national mean of 100. When socioeconomic class and housing tenure were allowed for, a 20–30% increase in mortality rate among the unemployed still remained. These figures were higher for younger and middle-aged men and could not be explained by other demographic characteristics such as marital status. The SMR for unemployed women and for women whose husbands were unemployed was 122 and 110, respectively. The SMR from all cardiovascular disease for the unemployed group was 117, but it was significantly higher for men aged 15–44. For this group the SMR for circulatory disease was 186, and for ischemic heart disease it was 216. There were similar significant increases in mortality rates for the wives of these workers.

Studies that have measured utilization of health services have reported increases in the frequency of visits to family physicians (D'Arcy 1986) and greater limitation on daily activities due to physical symptoms for both the unemployed themselves and their spouses (Fagin and Little 1984; Grayson 1985; D'Arcy 1986; Arber 1987). More frequent visits to a family physician may also represent attempts to find additional help or support to deal with problems being faced.

While preexisting symptoms may become more debilitating, other outcomes have been described. Fagin and Little (1984) examined the impact of unemployment on the health of members of 22 families in England and identified several possible courses. Preexisting health problems of unemployed males usually deteriorated, but in some cases they improved. This improvement occurred if the original problem was a manifestation of stress or of dissatisfaction with the job that had been lost, or if good health could facilitate a job search.

At a later stage, Fagin and Little found that there was

likely to be an increase in "psychosomatic" symptoms among both unemployed workers and their spouses, and more behavioral problems in their children. They postulated that these symptoms might be maintained because "it is better [more acceptable] to be sick and unemployed than healthy and unemployed for a jobless man in our society" (p. 117). The authors identified the meaning of a job, perceptions of societal attitudes toward unemployment, financial pressures, job opportunities, marital support, and the ability to occupy time as being important factors that contribute to the physical and emotional well-being of the unemployed and their families.

Mental Health

A consistent finding of studies of the impact of job loss has been an increase in emotional problems and symptomatology among jobless workers. This effect has been measured in three ways. The first has been from the subjective reports of the unemployed as to the changes they perceive and the distress they are experiencing. The second method has been to study changes in hospitalization rates. While these rates have fluctuated, it is often unclear whether this fluctuation reflects new cases or readmissions of individuals with preexisting problems that have been exacerbated. There may also be little information on the problem or diagnosis leading to the admission. And as previously discussed, hospitalization rates can depend on many other variables unconnected to job loss.

The third approach has been to use valid screening instruments or questionnaires such as the GHQ. These will identify changes in symptoms but not necessarily their severity. Many recent studies have included scales designed to measure specific symptoms such as depression or anxiety—the Beck Depression Inventory (BDI; Beck et al. 1961), for example—but researchers have not so far used instruments such as the Diagnostic Interview Schedule or the Present State Examination that might identify the presence of other major psychiatric disorders. As a result, although there is consistent evidence of decreases in overall satisfaction, general well-being, and self-esteem, and of increases in symptoms of depression, few conclusive findings exist as to the possible role of unemployment in the development of more severe psychiatric syndromes.

Diminished self-esteem has been a central finding in almost every study of workers who lose their jobs. Contributing factors include a sense of failure or shame, feelings of rejection, an individual's loss of control over his or her environment, the loss of work-related roles, the reaction of family and friends, and the attitudes in the worker's community. Increased symptoms of depression have also been identified as a frequent outcome of losing a job, not only by unemployed workers but also by their spouses.

Melville et al. (1985) used the BDI to compare changes in mood between employed and unemployed workers in Southampton, England. Although there were no statistically significant associations between age, sex, socioeconomic class, marital status, or decrease in income, the authors found a strong relationship between higher test scores and being out of work. Eighteen percent of unemployed workers—compared to 6% of employed workers—had scores above the threshold for the presence of a depressive disorder. Braithwaite and Garcia (1985), using the BDI to measure depression among young unemployed workers in England, came up with similar findings.

The symptoms of depression can also be moderated by the presence of social support. Bolton and Oatley (1987) conducted a longitudinal study of 49 recently unemployed men in England. The authors divided their sample into two groups: those who found new work and those who remained unemployed. They found that while 25% of the unemployed—but none of the reemployed—met the diagnostic criteria for a depressive disorder, higher levels of social support, as measured by a semistructured interview, played a significant role in reducing the symptoms of depression among the unemployed.

The same conclusion was reached by Brenner and Levi (1987), who conducted one of the few studies that has concentrated on the well-being of unemployed women. A 2-year study of 400 unemployed workers found that up to 40% of these individuals described pronounced depressive reactions, but that these reactions were less likely to occur in women with higher levels of social support.

A further inquiry of interest into the relationship between depression and unemployment was a cross-sectional study conducted by Dressler (1986) in a black community in the southern United States during a period of high local unemployment. Using regression analyses, Dressler concluded that unemployment caused increases in symptoms of depression independently from demographic factors and other stressors. The author also found that the impact of unemployment was exacerbated for families with low income and at times of high noneconomic life change.

Many of the studies of the impact of unemployment have found that symptoms peak between 3 and 6 months after the job is lost, and often disappear completely when new work is found. The onset of symptoms in a spouse usually takes place later than it does in the individual who loses a job. Many of these changes should probably be understood as a response to the stresses and losses experienced, although the changes may be more severe if other variables coexist. In the long run it may be other factors such as economic deprivation, diminished self-esteem, or family stress, which may even predate the loss of the job, that play an increasing role in the continuation of emotional difficulties.

Unemployment and Families

Spouses

Relatively few studies of the impact of unemployment have examined the effects on the spouses of workers who lose their jobs. Those that have done so have found that spouses are likely to experience many of the same effects as the individuals who have lost their jobs, including depression and anxiety, increased levels of stress, and deterioration in physical health

(Komarovsky 1940; Cochrane and Stopes-Roe 1981; Fagin and Little 1984; D'Arcy 1986; Grayson 1985; Atkinson et al. 1986; Smith 1985b; Penkower et al. 1988). In some instances, however, the well-being of wives has improved because they have enjoyed assuming a more responsible family role or have benefited from having to return to work themselves. Researchers have yet to examine the role of the social support system provided by the spouses in moderating the effects of job loss.

Children

Even less attention has been paid to the effects of unemployment on the children of the unemployed, although Fagin and Little (1984) described increased behavioral problems among a small sample. There is some evidence that children of the long-term unemployed are likely to be of lower birth weight, to be smaller, to have more health problems early in life (Macfarlane and Cole 1985; Margolis and Farrau 1981), and to do worse on tests of cognitive development (Department of Health and Social Security 1981; Chinnock et al. 1984), when compared with children whose parents are working. However, these effects may be hard to differentiate from those of poverty and poor nutrition, which frequently coexist.

Family Violence

Taitz and his colleagues carried out a study in Sheffield, England that examined the relationship between unemployment and child abuse (Taitz et al. 1987). They compared two cohorts of abused children seen in the same hospital, one between 1974 and 1979 (a period of low local levels of unemployment) and the other between 1980 and 1984 (a period of high local levels of unemployment). Although the number of children whose fathers were without work was proportionately higher in the second group, the increase in child abuse found was accounted for by an increase in the number of single-parent families and families whose resident male had never had a job.

There was no evidence to suggest that there was an increase in child abuse in families that had been stable prior to the loss of the job. The authors emphasize the need to distinguish families with preunemployment problems from those with stable family and work records prior to the worker losing his job.

Other studies have identified a link between unemployment and family violence, including spouse abuse (Nichols 1976). A survey of parents of 6,532 children registered with the National Society for the Prevention of Cruelty to Children in the United Kingdom between 1977 and 1982 identified the major precipitants of abuse as being unemployment, marital discord, family poverty and debts, and lack of self-esteem (Creighton 1984). Because unemployment can lead to the other three precipitants, it may play an important predisposing role in child abuse.

Family Breakdown

Unemployment has been linked with family breakdown. In 1979 in the United Kingdom the divorce rate was 34 per 1,000 for the unemployed and 15 per 1,000 for those who were working (Popay 1984). Burgoyne (1985) studied 100 English couples with the male being unemployed and found that 33% of the couples identified deterioration in their relationship compared to 3% of 100 cross-matched couples with the male being employed. This finding does not make a strong case for a direct causal relationship, but it does suggest that unemployment may be a contributing factor.

Unemployment and Suicide Rates

The correlation between unemployment and suicide rates has consistently been shown to be positive across different geographic areas, although it has not always proven to be statistically significant. Boor (1980) reported positive associations between suicide and unemployment rates between 1963 and 1976 in six out of eight countries studied. Recent evidence, however, suggests that the association of unemployment with both suicide and parasuicide (attempted suicide) is reduced markedly when the effects of poverty and psychotropic prescription rates are controlled for (Platt and Duffy 1986).

Platt and Kreitman (1985) carried out a long-term study of unemployment rates and parasuicide rates in Edinburgh, Scotland, and found the correlation to be positive from 1968 until 1982. From 1982 to 1984 the parasuicide rate began to decline even though unemployment rates were rising. The authors thought it possible that the figures represented an artifact, because fewer people who attempted suicide were admitted to a hospital compared to a decade earlier. There could also have been a reduction in the stigma or sense of alienation in losing a job at times of higher unemployment, because unemployed people were likely to have been better integrated within the social structure. These findings suggested that the psychological sequelae of unemployment could be less significant in areas that have become accustomed to high unemployment rates.

Micro level studies show a clearer association between unemployment and parasuicide, with parasuicide rates being significantly higher among the unemployed than among those who are working (Platt 1986). Platt and Duffy (1986) estimate that in up to 50% of parasuicides, the impact of unemployment could be a contributing factor. They recognize the difficulties in determining whether the impact of unemployment is a predisposing factor or a precipitating factor in suicide attempts. However, they believe that job loss should be seen as a predisposing factor because it leads to family stresses, changes in roles, and reduced self-worth, which in turn lead to suicidal behavior. They also point out that the percentage of parasuicides who are defined as "sub-employed" (i.e., who move in and out of the work force on a regular or seasonal basis) has decreased. This may mean that a greater proportion of the sub-employed are now permanently unemployed, which is consistent with the notion of an increase in structural unemployment (see Chapter 2).

Hawton and Rose (1986) reviewed the link between unemployment and parasuicide and reached a different conclusion. They believe that unemployment exaggerates or exposes factors known to increase the likelihood of suicidal behavior, such as interpersonal problems, poverty, and psychiatric disorders. They postulate that those who are psychologically vulnerable are more likely to become—and remain—unemployed and would be disproportionately represented among those having difficulty coping.

Unemployment and Other Social Indicators

Unemployment and Drug and Alcohol Use

Peck and Plant (1986) studied 1,036 young people in Scotland and found no association between unemployment and alcohol or tobacco use. Other researchers, including Iversen and Klausen (1986) in Denmark and D'Arcy (1986) in Canada, have confirmed this finding, postulating that the unemployed could no longer afford to drink as much as when they were working. Conversely, the United Kingdom General Household Survey in 1982 found a higher percentage of unemployed workers to be heavy drinkers compared to employed workers (Office of Population Censuses and Surveys 1984). Crawford et al. (1985) found that the unemployed drank the same quantity of alcohol but their drinking patterns changed. They were, for example, more likely to drink in binges and to experience more serious consequences from their drinking. In a Canadian study, Smart (1979) found that unemployed workers and shift workers were likely to drink more than those who were employed.

Peck and Plant (1986) also found a weak, but significant, association between unemployment and illicit drug use, a finding confirmed in a review of national data in the United Kingdom over a 14-year period (Crawford et al. 1985). This finding is consistent with those of other British and American studies (Borus 1984), although variables such as poor education and poverty also contributed to drug use by the unemployed.

Unemployment and Criminal Behavior

Gillespie (1975) reviewed 30 studies of the relationship between unemployment and criminal behavior. Although most studies demonstrated an association between the two, most criminal acts involved theft of property rather than personal violence, which could suggest economic need as being a contributing pressure. This association may not be as strong for women as for men (Borus 1984).

Demographic Factors Affecting the Outcome of Unemployment

Age

Older Workers

Most studies of plant closures have shown that it has proven harder for older workers to find new employment (Gordus et al. 1981; Hammerman 1964; Foltman 1968; Holen et al. 1981). Those who do find work often experience a greater loss of wages than do younger workers (Hammerman 1964). Many older workers eventually choose early retirement even though they would still prefer to work. One reason that has been suggested for these problems is age discrimination. Older workers may be perceived as less productive or harder to retrain. They are also seen as a poor long-term investment because they have fewer working years ahead of them, they require greater costs in pension contributions and accident insurance coverage rates, and they are more likely to take time off because of illness.

Seniority may also be a factor. Some workers are overqualified for jobs that are available, or are used to receiving a higher wage for performing the same work they are being offered. Ill-health may also affect older workers' participation in the work force or limit the kinds of work they can perform. In addition, senior responsibilities may make it harder for an employee to be absent from his or her job to look for new work before a plant closes.

Younger Workers

Younger people face different problems. Many younger people without jobs have never been part of the work force and as a result have been denied the opportunity to develop a sense of belonging to the adult world that working offers. They may, therefore, never have had a chance to internalize an image of themselves as a productive or valued worker.

A number of authors have described characteristic emotional and behavioral patterns in "school leavers" (both graduates and dropouts) who fail to find work (Stafford et al. 1980; Kosky 1980; Donovan and Oddy 1982). Initially school leavers may experience a sense of release from the regimentation of school, but this soon turns to frustration, resentment, or anxiety when they are unable to find work. The teenager begins to associate more with others in a similar predicament, feeling undervalued or excluded by the rest of the community. This increased sense of alienation, frustration, and hopelessness can be acted out, leading to antisocial or destructive behaviors or trouble with authority figures. It may also lead to the development of antisocietal attitudes that may be reinforced by peers and can make it progressively harder for the school leaver to integrate into the work force.

A longitudinal study of American workers over a 10-year period (Parnes 1982) found that a period of unemployment soon after leaving school was more likely to lead to further episodes of unemployment and to lower average earnings for the remainder of these individuals' working careers. Borus (1984) studied the labor market experiences of 12,500 Americans aged 18–22. He found that less highly educated and black school leavers were more likely to experience periods of joblessness and that school dropouts were three times more likely to be unemployed than high school graduates. Attending a private, rather than a public, school and receiving additional academic or vocational preparation were predictive of a more positive labor market outcome.

Stafford et al. (1980) studied 647 English school dropouts in one city. They found higher rates of unemployment among teenagers from the lowest socioeconomic classes, from families of West Indian descent, and from families where the father was unemployed, and among teenagers with the lowest levels of education.

These authors differentiated between factors that might affect an individual after losing a job and those that made it more difficult for a young person to find a first job after leaving school. They found that the young people at greatest risk of developing problems after losing a job were those with the highest commitment or motivation to work, although this was not a significant factor among those who were unable to find a first job.

Stafford et al. also addressed the question of work attitudes. When they compared their sample with a study of adults conducted by Warr et al. (1979), the teenagers sampled had a higher desire to work. Work involvement, closely connected to the meaning of a job, is clearly an important area for further research to predict who will have the most trouble coping with the loss of a job.

Feather and O'Brien (1986) conducted a cross-sectional study of Australian school leavers. They examined the moderating effect of (a) the need for employment, (b) the value placed on employment, and (c) personal ethics on the psychological well-being of employed and unemployed young people. Those school leavers who were unable to find a job saw themselves as less competent, less pleasant, and less active. These individuals reported more stress symptoms, more depression, less satisfaction with life, and had lower personal ethic scores. They rated their need for a job as less than the need of those who had found work. They also reported that they were less disappointed about being out of work.

These results indicated that group differences existed even before subjects attempted to join the work force and were maintained subsequently. Such differences were more likely to influence the likelihood of someone finding a job rather than moderating the impact of the experience of being unemployed.

Changes in employment status also affected the way individuals explained the reasons for their unemployment. For example, over time the loss of a job was likely to be accompanied by an increasing tendency for the individual to blame unemployment on social or economic (external) factors. There was also a decreased tendency to see a lack of motivation or interviewing inadequacies as contributing to the failure to find new work. These changes were reversed when the individual found a job.

This result contrasts with the finding of Warr et al. (1979), who noted a tendency for the opposite to occur in adults as the duration of the period of unemployment lengthened. Those individuals who initially saw their difficulties in finding work as originating with external factors started to see their problems more in terms of their own lack of competence or ability as time passed.

Level of Education

Another consistent finding has been that lower levels of education increase the difficulty in finding work after a job is lost (Foltman 1968; Dorsey 1967; Hammerman 1964). Indeed, a higher level of education and better qualifications lead to improved employment prospects at every stage of an individual's work career (Borus 1984). Lower educational levels frequently reflect other related impediments to reemployment such as lower socioeconomic class, poverty, or limited work skills. The lack of appropriate qualifications (high school diploma, university degree) may also lead to unemployed individuals being passed over for job interviews, thereby becoming a part of an impersonal screening process.

Literacy skills are also relevant. Many individuals who cannot read or write may, in a previous job, have relied upon verbal skills or memory to compensate for this lack of literacy skills. This may no longer be possible, especially if their new work involves the use of electronic equipment such as a computer, calculator, or even a supermarket till.

Race

A worker's race or color can also affect his or her employment prospects. Unemployment rates for blacks in Britain and the United States, especially for young people, have consistently been up to three times higher than those for whites with similar qualifications and backgrounds (Staples 1975; Parnes 1982). Palen and Fahey (1968) studied Studebaker workers laid off in South Bend, Indiana, and found that nonwhites had significantly higher unemployment rates at 4 months following the layoff, a finding corroborated by the Packard study (Aiken et al. 1969). Stern (1969) studied displaced meat packers in Kansas City and found that when these individuals were reemployed after a period of unemployment, blacks made an average of $204 per year less than whites.

The most common explanation for this discrepancy is racial discrimination and stereotyping, although immigrants may face additional handicaps if they are unfamiliar with job search procedures or opportunities. As with older workers, racial minorities may be seen as being less productive or harder to train. While these are misconceptions, they create additional obstacles for black and immigrant workers who are seeking employment.

Sex

Most studies of plant layoffs have focused on male-dominated plants or on male workers (i.e., production workers rather than secretaries). Nevertheless, those studies that have compared male and female workers have found female unemployment to be higher (Hammerman 1964) and of longer duration (Parnes 1982). A Canadian study of a plant closure in southern Ontario by Burke (1985) found that women experienced more severe economic consequences of losing their job, including shorter duration of subsequent employment, lower future earnings, and a greater drop in wages. And Stern, in his study of Kansas City meat packers (Stern 1969), found that when these individuals obtained further work after being unemployed, women would make an average of $2,123 per year less than males.

Women are also likely to experience age discrimination at an earlier stage than men. Hammerman (1964), in a review of five plant closures in five different industries, found that the peak level of unemployment for men occurred between the ages of 55 and 59, whereas for women it occurred between 45 and 54.

While women who are second wage earners may not always feel the same degree of urgency to work, discrimination again may be a factor that prevents them from finding a job. The issue of discrimination becomes more important as greater numbers of young mothers and sole-support parents, who may make additional demands on employers for child-care services or flexible time arrangements, are entering the work force. Potential employers may see these employees as more bothersome or expensive and overlook them in favor of other workers.

Socioeconomic Class

There is accumulating evidence of the link between lower socioeconomic status and health and mental health problems and life expectancy (Wilkinson 1986; Department of Health and Social Security 1980; Liem and Liem 1978). There are, however, many other factors associated with lower socioeconomic class that independently or collectively can have an effect on an individual's well-being, whether or not he or she is working.

The relationship between socioeconomic class and unemployment is complex. Workers from lower socioeconomic classes are more vulnerable to the effects of economic change and are more likely to lose their jobs than workers from higher socioeconomic classes. In addition, the effects of unemployment and the disadvantages faced by members of lower socioeconomic groups often reinforce each other. Many things happen to individuals who lose their job, and it can be difficult to differentiate between stress that has been caused by other factors and stress that has been exacerbated by the loss of a job. Socioeconomic factors may also increase the likelihood of an individual losing his or her job or make it harder to find new work.

In addition, a socioeconomic class is not a homogeneous group but is made up of individuals in many different situations (Kates and Krett 1988). Some individuals are upwardly mobile, and some are caught in a downward social drift. Some have grown accustomed to their predicament over many years, and some face temporary situations that lower their earning capacity or flexibility in finding a job, such as trying to look after young children. Some possess skills they will eventually be able to utilize, while others have fewer skills or abilities to increase their earning potential. When dealing with the impact of losing a job it may be important to differentiate between specific subgroups within a socioeconomic class that have varying degrees of vulnerability rather than to define everyone as being in the same predicament.

Although unemployment rates among professional workers remain lower than those for blue-collar workers, professional groups are not immune to economic fluctuations. In Toronto, for example, in the year after the stock market crash of October 1987, there was a net reduction of 10% in the total number of stockbrokers employed by firms that were members of the Toronto Stock Exchange (Toronto Globe and Mail 1989). Many professionals face equally severe long-term problems in adjusting to major decreases in earning potential or job responsibility or to changes in life-style (Greiff and Munter 1980). Those who are overly invested or defined by their work, who have extensive financial commitments that they are no longer able to maintain, or who are older and less likely to find equivalent work are at particular risk.

Jacobsen (1987) studied the effects of unemployment on 35 professional engineers in Massachusetts and identified two types of stressors that could lead to emotional difficulties. The first type were stressors that challenged or depleted an individual's resources or his or her ability to keep up with demands. On the whole, unemployed workers with few financial problems felt better and had fewer depressive symptoms than those who had preexisting economic problems. The second type were stressors related to the personal meaning of the job that had been lost, so that unemployment often led to a period of self-examination and a reappraisal of goals or professional identity.

The Disabled

Individuals who are physically or emotionally disabled face additional hardships in entering or reentering the work force. Once again, many of these hardships stem from employer or coworker prejudices, biases, or misconceptions.

For the physically disabled, including those with permanent impairments from work-related injuries, work options may be more limited, particularly among the lower-skilled jobs that require physical or manual labor. Many disabled employees adjust over time to a particular work setting that in turn makes changes to accommodate the worker. It may be difficult to find such flexibility when starting a new job. Positive discriminatory hiring policies can lead to the provision of jobs for the disabled, but these jobs often are menial and pay poorly, with little opportunity for advancement.

Interconnections Among Demographic Factors

Many of the above factors that can affect the well-being of individuals who lose a job may be interconnected. Older workers or migrants, for example, may have been less likely to have obtained educational qualifications that are comparable to those of recent nonmigrant graduates. It is often workers with multiple disadvantages who are at higher risk of developing emotional problems when they become unemployed.

Conclusions

The findings discussed in this chapter present conclusive evidence that a period of unemployment can have a major effect on the emotional well-being of individuals and their families. To help those who do lose their job, we first need to understand the personal impact of economic change and job loss, and the mechanisms whereby these changes are transmitted to an individual and his or her family and lead to emotional problems.

References

Ahr P, Gorodoezky M, Cho DW: Measuring the relationship of public psychiatric admissions to rising unemployment. Hosp Community Psychiatry 32:398–401, 1981

Aiken M, Ferman LA, Sheppard HL: Economic Failure, Alienation, and Extremism. Ann Arbor, MI, University of Michigan Press, 1969

Arber S: Social class, non-employment, and chronic illness: continuing the inequalities in health debate. Br Med J 294:1069–1073, 1987

Atkinson T, Liem R, Liem J: The social costs of unemployment: implications for social support. J Health Soc Behav 27:317–331, 1986

Bakke EW: The Unemployed Worker. New Haven, CT, Yale University Press, 1940

Baum A, Fleming R, Reddy D: Unemployment stress: loss of control, reactance and learned helplessness. Soc Sci Med 22:509–516, 1985

Beck AT, Ward CH, Mendelson M, et al: An inventory for measuring depression. Arch Gen Psychiatry 4:561–571, 1961

Bolton W, Oatley K: A longitudinal study of social support and

and depression in unemployed men. Psychiatr Med 17: 453–460, 1987

Boor M: Relationships between unemployment rates and suicide rates in eight countries, 1962–1976. Psychol Rep 47:1095–1101, 1980

Borgen W, Amundsen N: The Experience of Unemployment. Scarborough, Ontario, Nelson Canada, 1984

Borus M (ed): Youth and the Labor Market: Analyses from the National Longitudinal Study. Kalamazoo, MI, WE Upjohn Institute for Employment Research, 1984

Box G, Jenkins G: Time Series Analysis: Forecasting and Control. Oakland, CA, Holden Day, 1976

Braithwaite A, Garcia S: Depression in the young unemployed and those on Youth Opportunities Schemes. Br J Med Psychol 58:67–74, 1985

Brenner MH: Mental Illness and the Economy. Cambridge, MA, Harvard University Press, 1973

Brenner MH: Mortality and the national economy: a review, and the experience of England and Wales 1936–76. Lancet, Sept 15, 1979, pp 568–573

Brenner MH: Economic change, alcohol consumption and heart disease mortality in nine industrialized countries. Soc Sci Med 25:119–132, 1987

Brenner S, Levi L: Long-term unemployment among women in Sweden. Soc Sci Med 25:153–162, 1987

Bunn AR: Ischaemic heart disease mortality and the business cycle in Australia. Am J Public Health 69:772–781, 1979

Burgoyne J: Unemployment and married life. Unemployment Unit Bull, Nov 1985, pp 7–10

Burke R: Comparison of men and women following a plant shutdown. Psychol Rep 57:59–66, 1985

Catalano R, Dooley D, Jackson R: Economic predictors of admissions to mental health facilities in a non-metropolitan community. J Health Soc Behav 22:284–298, 1981

Catalano R, Dooley D, Jackson R: Economic antecedents of help-seeking: reformulation of time-test series. J Health Soc Behav 26:141–152, 1985

Chinnock A, Keegan PT, Fox PT, et al: Associations between growth patterns, social factors, morbidity and developmental delay in a longitudinal study of preschool children, in Human Growth and Development. Edited by Borns J. London, Plenum, 1984

Cobb S, Kasl S: Termination: the consequence of job loss. Report for the National Institute for Occupational Safety and Health Research (DHEW Publ No 77-224). Cincinnati, OH, U.S. DHEW, 1977

Cochrane R, Stopes-Roe M: Women, marriage, employment and mental health. Br J Psychiatry 139:373–381, 1981

Colledge M, Hainsworth M: Death on the dole: the impact of unemployment on health. Medicine in Society 5(3):15–22, 1982

Crawford A, Plant M, Kreitman N, et al: Self-reported alcohol consumption and adverse consequences of drinking in three areas of Britain: general population studies. Br J Addiction 80:421–428, 1985

Creighton S: Trends in Child Abuse. London, National Society for the Prevention of Cruelty to Children, 1984

D'Arcy C: Unemployment and health: data and implications. Can J Public Health 77 (suppl 1):124–131, 1986

Department of Health and Social Security: Inequalities in Health. London, Department of Health and Social Security, 1980

Department of Health and Social Security, Subcommittee on Nutritional Surveillance: Report of Health and Social Subjects. London, Her Majesty's Stationery Office, 1981

Donovan A, Oddy M: Psychological aspects of unemployment: an investigation into the emotional and social adjustment of school leavers. J Adolesc 5:15–30, 1982

Dorsey J: The Mack case: a study in unemployment, in Studies in the Economics of Income Maintenances. Edited by Eckstein O. Washington, DC, Brookings Institution, 1967

Dressler W: Unemployment and depressive symptoms in a southern black community. J Nerv Ment Dis 174:639–645, 1986

Eisenberg P, Lazarsfeld P: The psychological effects of unemployment. Psychol Bull 35:358–390, 1938

Eyer J: Does unemployment cause the death rate peak in each business cycle? Int J Health Serv 7:625–662, 1977

Fagin L, Little M: The Forsaken Families. London, Harmondsworth, UK, Penguin, 1984

Feather N, O'Brien G: A longitudinal analysis of the effects of different patterns of employment and unemployment on school-leavers. Br J Psychol 77:459–479, 1986

Fisher A: Psychiatric follow-up of long-term industrial employees subsequent to plant closure. Int J Neuropsychiatry 11:267–274, 1965

Foltman F: White- and Blue-Collars in a Mill Shutdown: A Case Study in Relative Redundancy. Ithaca, NY, ILR Press, 1968

Gillespie R: Economic Factors in Crime and Delinquency—A Critical Review of the Empirical Evidence—Final Report. Washington, DC, National Institute of Law Enforcement and Criminal Justice, U.S. Department of Justice, 1975

Gordus JP, Jarley P, Ferman L: Plant Closings and Economic Dislocation. Kalamazoo, MI, WE Upjohn Institute for Employment Research, 1981

Gore S: The effect of social support in moderating the health consequences of unemployment. J Health Soc Behav 19:157–165, 1978

Grayson JP: The closure of a factory and its impact on health. Int J Health Serv 15:69–93, 1985

Greiff B, Munter P: Tradeoffs: Executive, Family and Organizational Life. New York, New American Library, 1980

Group for the Advancement of Psychiatry: Job Loss—A Psychiatric Perspective. New York, Mental Health Materials Center, 1982

Hagen DQ: The relationship between job loss and physical and mental illness. Hosp Community Psychiatry 34:438–441, 1983

Hammerman H: Five case studies of displaced workers. Monthly Labor Rev 87:663–670, 1964

Hawton K, Rose N: Unemployment and attempted suicide among men in Oxford. Health Trends 18:29–32, 1986

Holen A, Jehn C, Trost R: Earnings Losses of Workers Displaced by Plant Closings. Alexandria, VA, Center for Naval Research, 1981

Iversen L, Klausen H: Alcohol consumption among laid off workers before and after closure of a Danish ship-yard: a 2 year follow-up study. Soc Sci Med 22:107–109, 1986

Jacobsen D: Models of stress and meanings of unemployment: reactions to job loss among technical professionals. Soc Sci Med 24:13–21, 1987

Jahoda M, Lazarsfeld PF, Zeisel H: Marienthal: The Sociography of an Unemployed Community. Chicago, IL, Aldine, Atherton, 1971

Justice B, Duncan D: Child abuse as a work-related problem. Correc Soc Psychiatry 23:53–55, 1977

Kates N, Krett E: Socio-economic factors and mental health problems: can census tract data predict referral patterns? Can J Community Ment Health 7:89–98, 1988

Komarovsky N: The Unemployed Man and His Family: The Effect of Unemployment Upon the Status of the Man in Fifty-Nine Families. New York, Dryden Press, 1940

Kosky R: Unemployment and the mental health of adolescents. Aust Fam Physician 9:845–848, 1980

Krugman R, Lenherr M, Betz L, et al: The relationship between unemployment and physical abuse of children. Child Abuse Negl 10:415–418, 1986

Lester D: Suicide and unemployment. Arch Environ Health 20:277–278, 1970

Liem R, Liem J: Social class and mental illness reconsidered: the role of economic stress and social support. J Health Soc Behav 19:139–156, 1978

Linn M, Sandifer B, Stein S: Effect of unemployment on mental and physical health. Am J Public Health 75:502–506, 1986

Macfarlane A, Cole T: From depression to recession—evidence about the effects of unemployment on mothers and babies health 1930's–1980's, in Born Unequal: Perspectives on Pregnancy and Childrearing in Unemployed Families. London, Maternity Alliance, 1985

Margolis L, Farrau D: Unemployment: the health consequences. NC Med J 42:849–850, 1981

Marsh L: Health and Unemployment. Oxford, UK, Oxford University Press, 1938

Melville D, Hope D, Bennison D, et al: Depression among men made involuntarily redundant. Psychol Med 15:789–793, 1985

Moser K, Fox A, Goldblatt P, et al: Stress and heart disease: evidence of associations between unemployment and heart disease from the OPCS Longitudinal Study. Postgrad Med J 62:797–799, 1986

Nichols B: The abused wife problem. Soc Casework 57:27–32, 1976

Office of Population Censuses and Surveys: General Household Survey 1982. London, Her Majesty's Stationery Office, 1984

Palen J, Fahey F: Unemployment and re-employment success: an analysis of the Studebaker shutdown. Ind Labor Relations Rev 21:234–250, 1968

Parnes H: Unemployment Experiences of Individuals Over a Decade. Kalamazoo, MI, WE Upjohn Institute for Employment Research, 1982

Peck D, Plant M: Unemployment and illegal drug use: concordant evidence from a prospective study and national trends. Br Med J 293:929–932, 1986

Penkower L, Bromet E, Dew M: Husbands' Layoff and Wives' Mental Health. Arch Gen Psychiatry 45:994–1000, 1988

Pilgrim Trust: Men Without Work. Cambridge, UK, Cambridge University Press, 1938

Platt S: Parasuicide and unemployment. Br J Psychiatry 149:401–405, 1986

Platt S, Duffy J: Social and clinical correlates of unemployment in two cohorts of male parasuicides. Soc Psychiatry 21:17–24, 1986

Platt S, Kreitman N: Parasuicide and unemployment among men in Edinburgh 1968–82. Psychol Med 15:113–123, 1985

Popay J: Unemployment and the Family. London, Unemployment Alliance, 1984

Smart RG: Drinking problems among employed, unemployed and shift workers. J Occup Med 21:731–736, 1979

Smith R: Bitterness, shame, emptiness and waste: an introduction to unemployment and health. Br Med J 291:1024–1028, 1985a

Smith R: "We get on each other's nerves": unemployment and the family. Br Med J 291:1707–1710, 1985b

Stafford E, Jackson P, Banks M: Employment, work involvement and mental health in less qualified young people. J Occup Psychol 53:291–304, 1980

Staples R: To be young, black and oppressed. Black Scholar 7(4):2–9, 1975

Statistics Canada: Duration of unemployment (table). Labour Force Information 39(6):67, 1983

Stern J: Evolution of private manpower planning in Armour's plant closing. Monthly Labor Rev 92(12):21–28, 1969

Strange WG: Report to the Manpower Administration, U.S. Department of Labor. Unpublished doctoral dissertation. Virginia Polytechnic Institute and State University, Blacksburg, VA, 1978

Taitz L, King J, Nicholson J, et al: Unemployment and child abuse. Br Med J 294:1074–1076, 1987

Thurlow HJ: Illness in relation to life situation and sick-role tendency. J Psychosom Res 15:73–88, 1971

Toronto Globe and Mail, Feb 4, 1989, B1

Ullah P, Banks M, Warr P: Social support, social pressures and psychological distress during unemployment. Psychiatr Med 15:283–295, 1985

Warr P: Twelve questions about unemployment and health, in New Approaches to Economic Life: Economic Restructuring, Unemployment and the Social Division of Labour.

Edited by Roberts B, Finnegan R, Gallie D. Manchester, UK, Manchester University Press, 1985

Warr P, Cook J, Wall T: Scales for the measurement of some work attitudes and aspects of psychological well-being. J Occup Psychol 52:129–148, 1979

Wilkinson R (ed): Class and Health: Research and Longitudinal Data. London, Tavistock, 1986

Winton M, Heather N, Robertson I: Effects of unemployment on drinking behavior: a review of the relevant evidence. Int J Addict 21:1261–1283, 1986

Chapter 4

*How the Effects
of Job Loss
Are Transmitted*

How the Effects of Job Loss Are Transmitted

Nothing to do with time; nothing to spend; nothing to
do tomorrow or the day after; nothing to wear; can't get
married. A living corpse; a unit of the spectral army of
the three million lost men.

Walter Greenwood *Love on the Dole*

*T*he accumulated findings of previous studies offer conclusive evidence that the loss of a job can lead to physical and
psychosocial problems. These problems occur through the direct effects of unemployment, by its impact upon the social
conditions of an individual, or by its role in exposing preexisting vulnerabilities or deficits.

There are, however, many intervening variables that can
play a role in determining the outcome of a period of unemployment. Conditions in the workplace, the availability of
social support, the quality of family relationships, financial
deprivation, and the reaction of the local community may all
influence the eventual outcome. There is also consistent evidence that among the most vulnerable are those individuals
who also face other social disadvantages, such as the poor, the
disabled, and members of racial minorities.

The effects of being unemployed also appear to change as
time passes and can be transmitted to an individual in many
different ways. To assist in the assessment and treatment of
individuals coping with the sequelae of losing a job, these different concepts need to be organized into an integrated
framework.

79

The first step in this process is to clarify the most significant effects of losing a job and look at how these are transmitted to an individual or his or her family. We can examine how these factors interact and then include other variables that may enhance or limit the severity of their impact.

The Ways Unemployment Affects an Individual

Many differing but complementary hypotheses have been put forward to explain the ways in which losing a job affects a person. These mechanisms are summarized below, although not every mechanism will be applicable in each individual case.

Losses

When the various benefits and advantages that work can offer are taken into consideration, it is clear that the termination of a job can lead to significant and substantive losses, although these will vary greatly from one situation to another.

In addition to the material deprivation discussed below, the loss of a job eliminates social contacts, friendship, and support that had been available within the workplace. There is often also a loss of daily structure that working brings. These losses cause feelings of sadness, anger, or guilt, which can in turn create a sense of isolation or alienation. If a worker is forced to relocate to find work or pursue a new career, he or she may have to leave behind friends, the local neighborhood, and a familiar environment in which he or she may have spent many contented years.

Someone who loses a job may be faced with multiple losses, the overall effect of which may be cumulative. While the impact of any one of these losses by itself may not be as severe as a bereavement, the initial process of adaptation and the stages of adjustment may be similar to a grieving process. Further losses may be encountered over a lengthy period of time, but their implications may not be fully appreciated until many weeks after the job has been lost.

Economic Deprivation

The financial losses may be particularly problematic. Indeed, many authors have suggested that the loss of a steady source of income and the lack of long-term security are the greatest hardships that unemployment brings (Aiken et al. 1969; Gordus et al. 1981; Jacobsen 1987). While the exact cost can be hard to assess, Howland (1988) has estimated that the average cost of a period of unemployment for an industrial worker in the United States between 1979 and 1982 was $1,285 for each year worked prior to the layoff, with a net reduction of $6.47 in weekly wages once the worker was reemployed. Unemployed workers who have access to additional material resources appear to cope better with the loss of their job and feel better about themselves (Jacobsen 1987). For those without such resources, the loss of an income may then lead to secondary losses if, for example, social activities have to be curtailed or possessions sold.

Changes in Roles

Changes in roles and role behaviors can be a useful way of conceptualizing the effects of losing a job. The work role can serve many different social and interpersonal functions. At one level the employer delegates clearly defined tasks and expectations that are part of a job description or title. These may be accompanied by spoken or unspoken assumptions as to behaviors associated with the position.

At another level, the interpersonal contacts that are an integral part of most jobs offer opportunities to meet psychological needs. Roles—and their associated behaviors—can shape, as well as reflect, an individual's internal identity, depending on the way in which others respond. Roles that encourage personal growth or creativity or that bring recognition and respect will enhance a person's self-esteem. Roles or role behaviors that are demeaning or stultifying can have the opposite effect.

The loss of the various roles and role activities a job provides is likely to be significant (Fried 1979). The absence of the recognition that accompanies a job can be distressing, altering individuals' views of themselves and undermining their self-esteem. To make up for this loss of a role, individuals may be forced to search for new or replacement roles in other parts of their life or adjust their behavior in existing relationships.

Changes in Self-Esteem

However resilient or self-assured an individual may be, losing a job or remaining unemployed can seriously undermine his or her self-esteem and sense of personal continuity. This process may begin with initial feelings of rejection or of being unwanted and may be reinforced by further rebuttals from unsympathetic employers or insensitive acquaintances. Negative comments from family members or those to whom an individual turns for help can add to a sense of inadequacy. Over time these changes in self-esteem can lead an individual to see himself or herself as being of lesser value as a person—a second-class citizen.

There is often a tendency for those who lose their job to blame themselves—usually unnecessarily—for what has taken place, portraying in an ever-worsening light their role in the unfolding of events over which they may have had no control. This self-blame promotes a further personal devaluation at a time when they may already be feeling unwanted by, or different from, the rest of the community. And for those whose job helped to define their identity, the loss of this job may lead to a crisis of identity and changes in self-image.

Increased Stress

There are many sources of stress for individuals who have lost a job. Stress can originate from increased environmental demands, which may exceed an individual's material resources or coping abilities, or from greater internal pressures as an individual's beliefs, values, and self-image are challenged.

82

One of the most immediate pressures is the need to find a new job. Some unemployed workers are fortunate. They possess marketable skills, they have contacts that lead to interviews, or they live in communities with numerous alternatives, any of which may help them find a new job within a short period of time. Others find the return to work to be a much tougher road. Each of the steps involved in finding work —appraising personal skills and strengths, searching out work opportunities, applying for jobs, and attending interviews— can be stressful. The pressures may increase as time passes, as personal hardships increase, and as the need to find work becomes more desperate. Many workers eventually reach a point where it seems futile to continue to apply for jobs or risk the disappointment of being rejected, and they give up the search.

Finding a new job may also involve additional expenses or even relocation to a new community. This can be particularly disruptive to family relationships, because other family members may have to stay behind until their relative is established in the new location. Moving may be even more stressful for an older worker, who may see limited work opportunities or feel less motivated to start a new career or move. By comparison, a younger worker with fewer family or material commitments who is just embarking upon a career may find it easier to attempt such a transition.

Unemployment can be stressful in other ways. Difficulties in applying for unemployment benefits are frequently encountered, with the bureaucratic procedures or the responses of staff who are perceived as being unsympathetic creating additional obstacles. The shame of dealing with a welfare agency may also prevent someone from utilizing resources that are available. If applying for social assistance becomes unavoidable, being treated with a lack of sensitivity or respect can reinforce a sense of inadequacy or failure.

Financial hardship is invariably a source of further stress, and budgetary adjustments may not be sufficient to make ends meet. Jobless workers are faced with the prospect of having to sell possessions or make major financial sacrifices to continue to honor their daily commitments. This also can reinforce a sense of failure and a diminished sense of self-worth, which in turn may impair the individual's ability to use the coping skills he or she possesses.

Changes in Social Support

Social relationships and community support are frequently disrupted when a job is lost. In part this disruption results from the loss of support and social contacts that were previously available within the workplace. Other contributing factors include a reduction in social activities due to limited finances; an avoidance of social contacts because of misperceptions of the attitudes of friends and former colleagues or because of a sense of shame or embarrassment at being unemployed; the termination of activities that were connected to the place of employment. The availability of support or resources within a community may also decrease at times of economic hardship or community disintegration.

A social support network refers to a complex set of interconnected relationships. The quality and quantity of these relationships and an individual's perceptions of their availability or of the attitude of others are all relevant. Indeed, the perception of support and its availability, rather than the support that actually exists, may be very significant in determining whether an individual avails himself or herself of such help.

The strength of a support network cannot be estimated solely by the number of contacts. It is important to look at an individual's needs, what he or she may be looking for, and what each contact offers. This requires a delineation of the component functions that a support system can serve. A social relationship can provide support, encouragement, friendship, contact, advice, material help (i.e., money), sanctuary, activities, and reassurance. Conversely, if a contact is critical, unsympathetic, or unhelpful, it can have a negative impact on someone in distress.

To appreciate how the loss of a social support network can

affect a person, it is necessary to understand the role this network plays and the ways in which it can help or hinder an individual's sense of well-being. Two differing but not exclusive views of the role of social support have been presented.

The first view is that participating in a social support network is an integral part of an individual's daily existence and activities. The presence of this support helps the development of coping skills, while its loss reduces opportunities for personal growth. At times of stress, therefore, a support network helps to reinforce the ability to cope with adversity.

The second view is that social support functions as a buffer. At times of hardship social supports directly reduce the effects of the stress, enabling an individual to utilize his or her resources to cope with new problems. Evidence from recent studies has emphasized the importance of this buffering role (Ullah et al. 1985; Bolton and Oatley 1987; Brenner and Levi 1987), while recognizing that enhancement of social skills is also a factor.

Changes in Family Relationships

The loss of a job will have an impact upon every member of a worker's family. One way that this can happen is through changes in the behavior of the unemployed individual that affect his or her family relationships. Someone who is depressed may be more short-tempered with, or withdraw from, other family members, while anxiety or stress may lead to reduced interest or involvement in family activities.

Other changes, such as adjustments in roles, may be more subtle. Individuals who were accustomed to an authoritarian role at work may begin to exaggerate those aspects of their role at home to compensate for the sense of self-importance they feel they have lost. Similarly, those individuals for whom the work role provided respect that they felt was denied them at home, may become more assertive or attention seeking in their interactions with their family.

In some situations a husband who was the primary wage

earner finds this role taken over by his wife or his child. This loss of role can be especially troubling for a man whose role within the family, as well as his identity and authority, may have been based on an ability to provide for his family, often through the fruits of his physical labor.

Families may also need to adjust to increased amounts of time spent together. In many instances this additional time spent together can have a beneficial effect, especially in the short-term, but this is not always the case. A homemaker may miss the time that she may previously have had for herself, seeing her husband as "invading" her territory during working hours. For other couples the lack of the outlet work provided may highlight communication problems or difficulties with intimacy.

The family is also affected by financial cutbacks. A spouse may be forced to return to work or take on an extra job to make ends meet. Children may be aware that they can no longer afford to buy clothes or toys or participate in activities with their friends that they had previously taken for granted.

The entire family may also be confronted with the stigma that can accompany unemployment. There may be a sense of shame or embarrassment at a family member being out of work, especially if the reaction of the local community is ambivalent or critical. Children may also become aware of "differences" between their parents and other working parents or may be subjected to ridicule by their peers. In many instances it is someone other than the unemployed worker who bears the brunt of these problems or who has to make the largest adjustment, or who becomes the one who copes or organizes for the family.

Unemployment should not, however, be seen as solely a negative experience for a family. It can bring members closer together as they support each other in facing a common threat or challenge. The additional time spent together can lead to greater intimacy and a strengthening of bonds. And there can be a shared sense of accomplishment when the family overcomes adversity and resolves its difficulties.

Uncovering of Preexisting Problems or Deficits

Preexisting deficits, whether physical, psychological, systemic, or interpersonal, can be exposed or uncovered by the loss of a job. Physical problems may deteriorate and make it harder for individuals to return to work, particularly if they are older. Workers with physical disabilities who had been able to adapt to one place of work may become more aware of the limitations of their disabilities when negotiating with a new employer. Health problems may also restrict the kinds of work that can be considered.

Underlying psychological problems include diminished confidence and self-esteem, poor coping skills, and more serious psychological or psychiatric disturbances. These problems may not have created difficulties when the individual was working in a relatively secure job and a predictable environment, but may become a factor when he or she has to cope with a new environment and possibly less-tolerant coworkers.

The symptoms of a psychiatric disorder may also be exacerbated. For some individuals, the increased stress and losses are sufficient to precipitate a further episode of the illness. Others may have experienced mild or subclinical symptoms of depression or anxiety due to general dissatisfaction with their life-style or relationships but found that work and its benefits compensated for this dissatisfaction. The loss of this counterbalance can accentuate the underlying symptoms. The challenges of adjusting to the loss of a job may also expose personal or interpersonal weaknesses or accentuate preexisting problems in family or marital relationships.

The term "uncovering" can also refer to the process of social labeling. Disadvantaged individuals whom a community may have tolerated and supported in times of greater prosperity may be redefined or labeled as problems or troublemakers as the economic situation worsens. As resources become more limited and competition becomes more intense, there may be less concern for the welfare of the disabled, who may then be forced from the work force.

An Integrated Model

The mechanisms described above are not exclusive. Indeed, they can be integrated into a simple model that highlights their interrelationships and demonstrates how problems or weaknesses in one area can lead to additional problems in other areas (see Figure 4–1). Protective factors reduce the impact of unemployment, or support or strengthen the individual. Provoking factors increase the impact of unemployment or make an individual more vulnerable. These factors are closely interconnected and are in a continuing state of flux. There are many ways of conceptualizing how these factors affect an individual, but changes in self-esteem are pivotal in most cases.

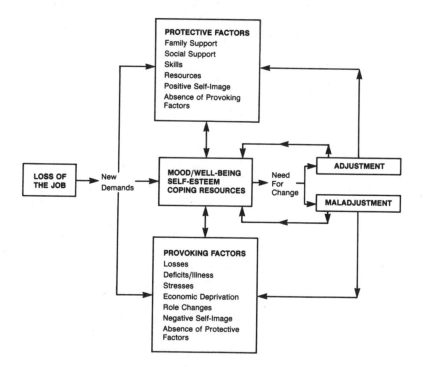

Figure 4–1. Factors affecting the outcome of losing a job.

The stress and losses of unemployment threaten an individual's ability to maintain a sense of personal continuity. Adjustments must be made to cope with the stress, increase social support, manage the changes, and continue with day-to-day activities. If these adjustments are successful they will reinforce the positive (protective) factors, increasing an individual's sense of self-confidence or self-esteem and helping him or her manage, even if new work is not found immediately. If these adjustments are not successful, there is likely to be an increase in the stresses and pressures, with a diminishing sense of self-effectiveness or worth and a restriction in the range and flexibility of roles, leading to further problems and internal distress.

To understand the impact of losing a job, an appreciation of these mechanisms is essential. There are, however, three other sets of factors that can contribute to the outcome and that need to be added to this framework. These factors are the personal significance or meaning of a job, the stages the individual passes through after losing a job, and the personal and environmental factors that can moderate or exaggerate the way the loss of the job is experienced.

Meaning of a Person's Work

As well as providing financial rewards, a job also fulfills social and psychological needs. Carlyle (1886) described work as "the grand cure for all the maladies and miseries that ever beset mankind." Freud (1930) saw work as man's strongest tie to reality, with the ability to work and to love being the central issues in life. To understand why losing a job can have such a profound effect, it is necessary to appreciate the personal meaning of what may have been lost.

Economic Meaning

The remuneration work provides pays for the essentials for day-to-day survival such as food and shelter, as well as additional "luxury" items that can make life more comfortable. It also enables a worker to purchase material symbols and possessions that can increase social standing or status and allow him or her to participate in leisure or social activities. Frequently, work also provides longer-term financial security through a pension, supplementary income after retirement, or opportunities to save money.

Social Meaning

Work relationships offer opportunities for friendship, support, and social contact, or they may be an escape from a dissatisfying family or personal life. Work can also provide a place and group to which an individual can belong and gain acceptance, and enable the worker to assume a clearly defined role and identity that can extend beyond the workplace. In social settings, many people choose to define themselves by their job or their work role. Talking about work can also establish fixed points or common ground in new interpersonal situations, especially at times when an individual may be feeling unsure or vulnerable.

Work serves another function: it breaks up the hours in the day. If leisure is defined as the time spent not working, without work there can be no leisure. And to a large extent work and work behavior form the basis of societal organization.

Psychological Meaning

Psychologically, work serves many functions. It may offer opportunities for expressing creative abilities, developing a sense of competence or mastery, accepting responsibility, recognition, and respect, all prerequisites for healthy emotional development.

Work also helps to form and preserve an individual's internal identity, self-worth, and sense of personal continuity, especially if the role is seen to have purpose and value.

Behaviors and interactions that are part of the work role are internalized and become an integral part of a self-image. Positive work experiences, recognition by peers or superiors, and the mastering of new challenges help to enhance this self-image. Conversely, negative experiences, insufficient stimulation, or a lack of respect from peers may diminish an individual's self-esteem or lead to an emotional "distancing" from his or her work.

For those who are not working, the same principle applies. Being unemployed is characterized by certain role behaviors and expectations, many of which are passive or dependent. Over time the experiences of being seen as unemployed are also internalized, leading to one of the consistent aftereffects of losing a job—changes in self-esteem.

Other psychological factors are also relevant. The work ethic is instilled from birth, and productive labor is held up as a social ideal. Work roles are modeled by those individuals whom children look up to, and these roles are consistently reinforced in the educational experiences and the culture to which these children are exposed, such as the stories they read.

For the teenager, working is a rite of passage in the transition from childhood to adulthood and from school to employment. Working promotes the establishment of a separate identity, while the wages earned often can be used to support a more independent life-style or allow a physical move away from the family of origin.

Despite the advantages working can bestow, not every job is capable of meeting an individual's needs. Work can be stultifying, stressful, demeaning, and exploitative. In these cases, losing a job may be a relief or an escape. For some, being laid off provides an opportunity to pursue alternate career plans. It may challenge them to find a job that is better suited to their talents or offer an outlet for previously untapped abilities. In general, however, the loss of a job entails multiple material, social, and emotional losses, and the greater the investment in the job, the greater the effects of the losses.

Stages of Unemployment

The majority of unemployed individuals eventually adjust to the loss of a job, make necessary changes, and find new work. For some, however, the despair and helplessness of being unemployed will continue for months or years, with little hope for the future.

The responses of those individuals who remain without work change over time, as do the issues and problems they have to deal with. Two ways of looking at these changes have been put forward. The first perspective identifies the different stages that someone will pass through after the job is lost and the challenges he or she will face in each phase. The second likens being unemployed to a roller coaster ride of emotional highs and lows in response to events and situations encountered.

A number of authors have identified the different phases of becoming unemployed (Harrison 1976; Powell and Driscoll 1973; Hopson and Adams 1976; Borgen and Amundsen 1984; Kirsh 1983). They have used different terminology but have described similar adjustments and challenges.

Harrison (1976) describes a journey that begins with the shock and passes through stages of optimism and pessimism before the final phases of adaptation to a lower living standard, fatalism, and despair. Powell and Driscoll (1973) studied a group of skilled and professional workers and defined the stages as being initial relaxation and relief, concerted effort, vacillation and doubt, and finally malaise and cynicism.

Hopson and Adams (1976) describe seven intermediate steps: initial immobilization, minimization, depression, acceptance, testing, and, finally, a search for meaning and the internalization of the new reality. These steps are similar to the stages described by Borgen and Amundsen (1984), who identify eight steps, the first four of which are derived from Kubler-Ross's model of grieving—denial, anger, bargaining, and depression—and reflect the job-loss grieving process. The later stages—enthusiasm, stagnation, frustration, and apathy—reflect the job-search burnout process.

The idea of the roller coaster has been superimposed on the concept of stages by Kirsh (1983) and by Borgen and Amundsen. During each stage an individual will experience a number of highs and lows, usually in response to external events. Beginning a job search may be a time of optimism, leading to a "high"; whereas being rejected by a potential employer or having to apply for welfare may be a depressing event, ushering in a "low" period.

We have summarized the stages of adjustment to losing a job as follows: anticipation, impact, activity and frustration, and the unemployed state.

Anticipation

The period of anticipation, overlooked by many authors, is important not only because it is the time when the emotional reaction begins, but also because it is a period when appropriate preparations and interventions can be effective in changing the outcome of job loss.

Workers may sometimes receive advance warning that their plant is to close or that they are to lose their jobs. This allows them to make preparations for what may follow or even to start a job search. In most instances, however, there is little advance warning or notice, particularly when it is only a small group of workers who are to be affected.

The anticipation stage can be a time of great anxiety and confusion, creating a sense of powerlessness or increased dependency. The result can be that extra demands are made on family and friends who may be unaware of what is taking place. Workers are often angry at what has happened to them but may have few outlets to ventilate this anger. The employer may be a remote or impersonal multinational corporation, or immediate superiors may themselves be in danger of losing their jobs, while "acting out" may jeopardize opportunities to receive severance pay. For many workers this period is also a time for self-recrimination and blame.

Some workers deal better with the stress and uncertainty;

they accept the inevitable and prepare themselves for what they believe is to come. Some start to work harder in the hope that they will make themselves indispensable to their employer, even volunteering for additional duties. Some, however, choose to deny the reality of their situation, refusing to accept that their job is at risk or believing that they will have no trouble in finding new work. A reluctance to make short-term adjustments or practical preparations during this period can have serious consequences after the job is lost.

Even before a closure or layoff is announced, there may be other sources of stress. In many workplaces rumors abound during this period, generating fear and uncertainty among all who might eventually be affected. This fear and uncertainty can increase competition and reduce solidarity and support among the work force, especially if some workers are privy to information that is denied others. It can also lead to a discrepancy within the workplace if upper management is aware of an impending closure and starts to plan for its own future while the rest of the work force remains unaware of what is taking place.

Impact

The reality of the loss of a job usually creates a personal crisis. The losses, the immediate stress, and the uncertainty can lead to sadness, anxiety, and a sense of helplessness. Feelings of indignation and resentment at the treatment received may fan the flames of anger but may also bring home the realization that the worker is relatively powerless and has lost a degree of control over a part of his or her life. There may also be strong feelings of guilt, shame, or failure from the worker's belief that he or she has let his or her family down.

The need to maintain or save face in other aspects of daily life can become exaggerated and reduce flexibility in dealing with new situations. It may also reduce the ability to utilize available help. There are many anecdotal reports of workers who having lost their job, continue to pretend to friends and relatives that they are still working. They leave home each day at the same time—dressed in their work clothes—and return at the accustomed hour each evening, spending the time in between searching for new work. If these individuals are successful, they can then let others think they are leaving their original job of their own free will.

Some workers respond in quite a different way. They see the immediate period after the job is lost almost as a "honeymoon," particularly if there are no pressing financial problems. They are confident about returning to work, so they use their free time to relax or to catch up on household tasks. Frequently, however, this confidence is misplaced and may serve only to postpone an inevitable period of crisis. The honeymoon may come to an abrupt end when it finally becomes apparent that finding new work will not be easy.

A relatively small group of workers are overwhelmed at this stage. The losses, the blow to their pride, or the sudden alienation from friends and peers can lead to severe symptoms of anxiety or depression and occasionally to a suicide attempt in response to a sudden sense of isolation and abandonment.

Activity and Frustration

In the ensuing months after the job is lost, the initial crisis begins to settle and a multitude of practical issues must be resolved. Finances need to be put in order, commitments reviewed, and necessary budgetary cutbacks made. The search for a new job must also begin, often with a reappraisal of abilities, strengths, and goals. It is a time of ups and downs, of hopes raised and dashed. But the more the bills pile up and the frustration mounts, the greater the uncertainty about the future becomes. A lack of success in finding work may reinforce a sense of failure or diminished self-worth and increase feelings of a loss of control. In many ways this period is characterized by a series of small crises, whose impact may be cumulative.

All of these factors can lead to increased feelings of anger and anxiety. The anger may be turned inwards, creating further self-recrimination and guilt. Events that led to the loss of the job may be reevaluated, with the worker portraying his or her role in an increasingly negative light. Anxiety may progressively erode the self-confidence necessary for a successful job search. It can also cause an individual to avoid situations that previously could have been handled or where support and assistance could be found. Alternatively, anger may be turned outward and result in a lower tolerance for frustration or personal setbacks. This reduced tolerance can increase the likelihood of temper outbursts, physical violence, and antisocial behavior.

The Unemployed State

Within 6 to 9 months of the loss of a job, many of the immediate practical difficulties may have been dealt with and new ways found to earn a living or cope with the predicament. Many unemployed people, however, continue to encounter problems in finding work while the stress continues. By this time contact with friends and supports may have been lost, the sense of rejection may be stronger, and feelings of isolation and alienation from the rest of the community may be heightened. Being unemployed becomes an increasingly prominent part of these individuals' daily existence and is gradually internalized, shaping their identity and self-image. They are now prepared to accept second best for themselves and their families as helplessness turns to hopelessness and anger to despair.

The transition from receiving unemployment insurance benefits to going onto social welfare marks a significant psychological turning point in this process. Unemployment insurance is something that most individuals feel they have earned through their work and contributions over the years. However, having to accept welfare represents a need to be taken care of and can be construed as a statement of dependency or failure.

This stage may be a time of reappraisal as the individual comes to terms with new life directions. It is a time when relationships face additional strains and families may separate. It may also be the point at which the worker decides he or she no longer has the energy to cope or to continue to look for work and becomes resigned to his or her fate.

Key Intervening Variables

Previous studies and our own clinical experiences have demonstrated that for each individual there are a number of additional factors, discussed below, that can affect the outcome of a period of unemployment. Some are protective, while others lead to additional stress and losses or make it likely that further problems will follow.

Personal Factors

In addition to age, sex, race, level of education, and socioeconomic class, three other groups of personal variables may need to be considered: psychological factors, material resources, and previous experiences of unemployment.

Other than self-esteem, qualities that can help an individual cope with the loss of his or her job include cognitive skills, problem-solving abilities, and the ability and flexibility to integrate and utilize new information. Interpersonal skills and the capacity to establish new relationships can also assist a job search, as can material resources such as job skills, literacy, contacts in the community, and, perhaps above all, financial stability and additional funds for use in emergencies.

Attitudes toward work and working are also relevant. The greater an individual's work commitment, or the more he or she disparages others who are not working, the harder it may be to come to terms with difficulties in finding new work. Previous job changes can also affect the way an individual copes. This applies not only to the loss of a job but also to situations in which workers have been demoted or have seen younger workers overtake them (Ferman and Gardner 1979). These groups of workers are more likely to experience periods of unemployment and to have greater difficulty coping and returning to work.

97

Workplace Factors

Workplace factors affecting the outcome of unemployment include the availability of support and resources to help workers prepare themselves and find new work, and the quality of the relationship between the employee and the employer. In general, the greater the attachment to the place of employment, the harder it may be to cope when a job is lost. The degree of forewarning received is also important, because advance notice offers a chance for the worker to make adjustments before the job, and paycheck, disappear.

The manner in which the job was lost is also relevant. Of the nine million Americans who were unemployed in October 1988, approximately 50% had been recently laid off or fired, while 25% were trying to reenter the work force after a longer period out of work. Of the remainder, half had chosen to leave their jobs and half were new entrants to the labor force (U.S. Department of Labor 1988).

For many reasons there are likely to be differences in outcome between a worker who is laid off and one who is fired because of poor performance, between one who loses his or her job involuntarily and one who chooses to leave, and between one who is laid off with the prospect of returning and one who is made redundant by the closure of an entire plant. The experience may also be different if a relatively small number of workers are laid off rather than the majority of a work force.

Family Factors

Many aspects of family life will have a bearing on the way an individual copes with the loss of his or her job. One such factor is the stage of the family life cycle that a family unit has reached. Families who are trying to establish themselves as a unit or who are adjusting to the arrival or departure of children may have less time or energy to cope with additional pressures than a more mature, settled family.

98

A family's financial state prior to the loss of the job will also invariably affect the outcome. Other factors to consider include the presence of alternative wage earners and the availability of extrafamilial or extended family support.

Social and Community Factors

The ability to occupy time productively, in social relationships or in personal activities, is very important (Hepworth 1980). Factors influencing this ability can include the availability and accessibility of a support network, an individual's perception of the availability of this support, his or her satisfaction with the role he or she has within a support system, and the cost of social activities or of maintaining memberships.

The existence of alternative work options and support programs for the unemployed within a community can provide increased opportunities to retrain or prepare for new work. The ease with which health and welfare benefits can be obtained is also crucial. Restrictive eligibility criteria for unemployment benefits may exclude many needy workers, while the availability of medical insurance coverage can determine whether or not an individual utilizes necessary health services.

Community attitudes can also affect long-term outcomes. If unemployment is a problem to which a community has grown accustomed, or if a large number of workers are unemployed, support and understanding may be more forthcoming than if only a few individuals are affected, or if dealing with the unemployed is a new experience for the wider community.

References

Aiken M, Ferman LA, Sheppard HL: Economic Failure, Alienation, and Extremism. Ann Arbor, MI, University of Michigan Press, 1969

Bolton W, Oatley K: A longitudinal study of social support and depression in unemployed men. Psychiatr Med 17: 453–460, 1987

Borgen W, Amundsen N: The Experience of Unemployment. Scarborough, Ontario, Nelson Canada, 1984

Brenner S, Levi L: Long-term unemployment among women in Sweden. Soc Sci Med 25:153–162, 1987

Carlyle T: Inaugural Address at Edinburgh University, 1886, in Familiar Medical Quotations. Edited by Strauss M. Boston, Little, Brown, 1968

Ferman L, Gardner J: Economic deprivation, social mobility and mental health, in Mental Health and the Economy. Edited by Ferman L, Gordus J. Kalamazoo, MI, WE Upjohn Institute for Employment Research, 1979, pp 193–224

Freud S: Civilization and Its Discontents (1930), in The Standard Edition of the Complete Psychological Works of Sigmund Freud, Vol 21. Translated and edited by Strachey J. London, Hogarth Press, 1955

Fried M: Role adaptation and the appraisal of work related stress, in Mental Health and the Economy. Edited by Ferman L, Gordus J. Kalamazoo, MI, WE Upjohn Institute for Employment Research, 1979, pp 139–192

Gordus JP, Jarley P, Ferman L: Plant Closings and Economic Dislocation. Kalamazoo, MI, WE Upjohn Institute for Employment Research, 1981

Harrison R: The demoralizing experience of prolonged unemployment. Canadian Department of Employment Gazette, April 1976, pp 339–348

Hepworth S: Moderating factors of the psychological impact of unemployment. J Occup Psychol 53:139–145, 1980

Hopson B, Adams J: Towards an understanding of transition: defining some boundaries of transition dynamics, in Transitions. Edited by Adams J, Hayes J, Hopson B. London, Martin Robertson, 1976

Howland M: Plant Closings and Worker Displacement. Kalamazoo, MI, WE Upjohn Institute for Employment Research, 1988

Jacobsen D: Models of stress and meanings of unemployment: reactions to job loss among technical professionals. Soc Sci Med 24:13–21, 1987

Kirsh S: Unemployment: Its Impact on Body and Soul. Toronto, Canadian Mental Health Association, 1983

Powell D, Driscoll P: Middle-class professionals face unemployment. Society 10(2):18–26, 1973

Ullah P, Banks M, Warr P: Social support, social pressures and psychological distress during unemployment. Psychiatr Med 15:283–295, 1985

U.S. Department of Labor, Bureau of Labor Statistics: Unemployed persons by reason for unemployment, monthly data seasonally adjusted (table). Monthly Labor Rev 111(8):69, 1988

Chapter 5

Assessing the Impact of Job Loss

Chapter 5

Assessing the Impact of Job Loss

> I don't like work—no man does—but I like what is in
> work—the chance to find yourself, your own reality, for
> yourself not for others—what no other man can ever
> know.
>
> Joseph Conrad *Heart of Darkness*

*T*he difficulties encountered by a worker who has lost his or
her job can come to the attention of a psychiatrist or mental
health service in various ways. Sometimes the problems or
symptoms are of such severity that help is sought through a
direct contact or by a referral from another professional or service assisting the individual. In these cases unemployment has
usually been identified as a major stressor and should become
a focus of any assessment. The challenge for the therapist is to
identify the ways in which the loss of the job has affected the
individual, assess the impact of these changes, and develop a
comprehensive management plan.

Alternatively, someone may present at a treatment setting
without recognizing that his or her symptoms could be connected to job loss, especially if the loss of the job occurred
many months previously. The presenting symptoms may be
physical or psychological and could be a new problem or an
exacerbation of a preexisting difficulty. The symptoms themselves may be vague and nonspecific, but their presence suggests an underlying problem that may not have been identified
or articulated.

In other situations a relative of someone who is unemployed, most commonly a spouse, may present with symptoms

of distress or illness that bear a temporal relationship to the job loss. Because the stress and pressures caused by unemployment are transmitted to the family system, they may have an even greater impact on other family members than on the person who is jobless. The underlying problem may be caused by a change in the behavior of the unemployed person, by excessive demands that are affecting his or her family, or by major alterations in activities or life-style because of a changing economic situation. The symptoms may serve to bring the plight of the family to the attention of caretakers, acting as a warning signal when no other method seems to work.

If the loss of the job has not already been identified as a factor contributing to the problem, the therapist faces the additional challenge of making the connection between the loss of the job and the onset of the presenting complaint by evaluating an assortment of personal and environmental factors.

It is safe to assume that almost everyone who loses a job will face some related problems and difficulties, however short the period of unemployment. Often these problems resolve spontaneously or require little more than support and information on available resources. Bringing the problem into the open, recognizing it, and validating the reality of the predicament may be sufficient, especially if little can be done instrumentally to improve the situation. The therapist, therefore, should always be alert to the possible effects of the loss of a job.

Guiding Principles

Some guiding principles should be followed when assessing an individual presenting with problems in which unemployment may be a factor.

1. The response of an individual worker to losing his or her job will be unique. The experience has to be understood in terms of the individual's previous experiences, his or her strengths and weaknesses, and his or her perceptions of what is happening. An essential part of this understanding

is appreciating the meaning of the job that has been lost, the benefits it provided, and the needs it met.

2. The different parts of an individual's life are in a delicate balance. Changes in one area will affect every other area as adjustments are made to establish a new equilibrium. Job loss, therefore, has the potential to affect any aspect of an individual's life and relationships. The impact of job loss on family relationships and social activities must be explored.

3. The effects of losing a job and the issues and problems that have to be dealt with change over time. The therapist should be aware of the stages that must be negotiated so that interventions are relevant to the current problems and the tasks of the stage that has been reached.

4. Multiple moderating factors can protect or expose an individual to the impact of job loss and affect the way problems are defined or how they present. A psychiatric assessment must be comprehensive, with a careful analysis of the factors in an individual's workplace, family, or community that may be contributing to the onset or continuation of the problems. These factors may also become the target of specific interventions.

5. The therapist must be familiar with a range of treatment and intervention options and cognizant of the possible roles—and the limitations—of psychiatric services when working with the unemployed. To achieve this perspective the therapist needs to be aware of the role of community and social agencies that provide services that may be of use to the unemployed, such as vocational programs, emergency shelters, and legal clinics. He or she must also know how to utilize or refer to these agencies and be able to work with them in a collaborative fashion.

The assessment approach described (outlined in Figure 5–1) follows these principles and builds upon the framework presented earlier (see Figure 4–1). This assessment has three areas: the individual, family relationships, and social and community activities.

107

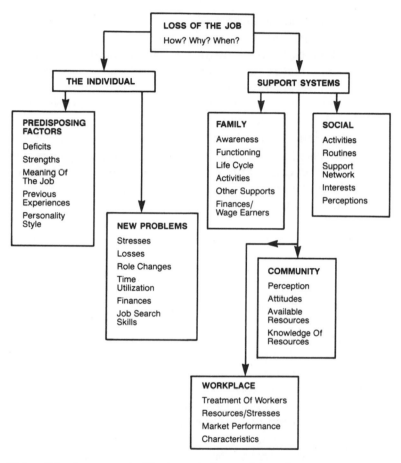

Figure 5-1. Assessment of the impact of unemployment.

Assessment of the Individual

Factors Relating to the Workplace or Job

The first step is to assess the importance of an individual's job and what working may have meant to him or her. To assist in eliciting this information, the therapist can inquire about the

length of the individual's working day, the amount of overtime worked, the reasons for working, the degree to which the job fulfilled long-term goals or ambitions, the stressors encountered on the job, and the extent to which work may have interfered with family or social activities. It is also worth inquiring about overall job satisfaction, attitudes toward people who do not work, the impact of the loss of the role(s) that work offered, and what is being done to compensate for this loss.

It is necessary to understand how the job was lost. There can be a big difference in the emotional responses to being fired, being laid off, being made redundant by the closure of an entire plant, or being unable to reenter the work force months or years after having chosen to leave a job.

Personal Deficits or Preexisting Problems

An accurate assessment of preexisting problems or deficits can be helpful in predicting problems that might emerge and in identifying those individuals who are likely to be at greatest risk. Problems or deficits that might hinder progress include limited coping skills, limited material resources, limited work skills, physical health problems, and more severe psychiatric problems.

Coping Skills

The ability to cope with the stress and problems of unemployment may be severely impaired by underlying psychological deficits. These deficits can include limited interpersonal skills, low self-confidence, a reduced capacity to handle disappointment or loss, cognitive problems or intellectual impairment, and poor problem identification and problem-solving abilities. While any of these can increase an individual's vulnerability, a lack of confidence or low self-esteem may be a particular handicap, because many of the events associated with losing a job can reinforce feelings of failure or inadequacy.

Limited Material Resources

The relative importance of economic deprivation as a factor contributing to the outcome of losing a job may be debatable. It is clear, however, that workers with fewer financial resources prior to job loss or those who are forced to make major economic cutbacks have a harder time coping with unemployment. It is worth inquiring about difficulties that predated the loss of the job as well as major changes or adjustments that have occurred subsequently. Financial commitments such as mortgage or loan payments that might be increasingly hard to maintain also need to be taken into account.

Work Skills

Assessing work skills requires more than simply asking the individual what he or she can, or would like, to do. Not only do specific skills and strengths need to be assessed, but their value needs to be understood in the context of the local availability of work. The assessment should also cover job search skills and a preparedness to retrain or relocate if that becomes necessary. Limitations in any of these areas can hinder the search for new work.

Poor Health

Problems with physical health will invariably impede attempts to find new work, especially in the case of those individuals who are older. In many cases a physical ailment that had been relatively untroublesome might become a problem for the first time. For example, someone with a back or knee injury who loses a sedentary job may find that the injury becomes more of a handicap when faced with the prospect of having to perform manual labor. Sometimes the opposite can occur, as preexisting health problems improve or are downplayed when the need to find work becomes paramount. A realistic health appraisal or a new treatment approach may help guide an unemployed worker toward a more appropriate or manageable job.

Preexisting Psychiatric Disorders

Although unemployment is not always thought of as one of the consequences of having a major psychiatric illness, the majority of individuals who are disabled by a psychiatric illness are unable to find or hold competitive jobs. Many psychiatric patients have been unemployed for lengthy periods of time, interspersed with brief but unsuccessful attempts to return to the work force. They face multiple problems when contemplating a return to work and are likely to need continuing support from rehabilitation programs or case managers.

Two other obstacles may have to be overcome. The first is that a history of emotional problems may have a negative effect on the attitude of a potential employer because of the stigma attached to psychiatric illness. The second obstacle involves individuals receiving disability benefits who may be faced with the loss of their pension—and the perceived security it offers—if they take a job that they may not in the long run be able to handle. These individuals then run the risk of finding themselves without either a job or a pension.

The Individual's Strengths

An assessment of an individual who is unemployed must include a careful examination of personal strengths, resources, and supports. Although the latter will include family and community supports, three other areas should be reviewed: psychological strengths and coping skills, material resources, and work skills. Many aspects of these areas have already been discussed above. Strengths are frequently the opposite of factors that increase a person's vulnerability. It can be extremely beneficial to ask the worker to list his or her strengths and skills, pointing out how few of these have been affected by the loss of

111

the job. This kind of approach can enhance a sense of personal continuity as well as point to possible solutions to particular problems. The value of other resources, such as owning a means of transportation, personal contacts, and knowledge of community supports that could help the search for work, should also be identified.

Impact of Losing a Job

The therapist must recognize and understand the emotional response to what has taken place. Anger, anxiety, fear, and sadness may each be an appropriate reaction at different stages of the process of coming to terms with new realities. The therapist should also be alerted to the possibility of a more serious problem if the affective response appears to be out of proportion to the event that provoked it or if the affect remains unchanged even though day-to-day pressures may be decreasing. When assessing affective responses it is helpful to remember the stages of unemployment through which an individual will pass and their impact on him or her.

It is also essential to differentiate between the actual and the perceived impact of the loss of the job. Specific questions should aim to elicit information on the accuracy of the perceptions of what has taken place; any recrimination, self-blame, and guilt felt for events that may have been beyond the worker's power to change; and any perceived loss of control.

Previous Experiences of Unemployment

Two areas may be relevant. The first concerns incidents that may have taken place during previous episodes of unemployment and the types of problems encountered. These experiences may present clues as to difficulties that might now arise, as well as to the kind of assistance that might be beneficial.

The second area involves the effects that previous experiences of unemployment have had on attitudes toward being out of work. Pessimism, a sense of loss of control, or fatalistic acceptance may all be detrimental to the longer-term ability to cope.

Family Factors

When an individual is out of work and facing problems, a family assessment should be considered. The assessment itself may be an effective intervention because it encourages family members to sit together and discuss their problems. It will also broaden the therapist's understanding of the family, often adding previously unsuspected information. A family assessment should also be considered when the individual who presents is someone other than the unemployed individual.

The family assessment should cover the following:

- Family members' awareness of one another's problems
- Family functioning as a unit or system
- Stage of the family life cycle that the family has reached
- Family activities
- Supports for the family
- Financial situation
- Other wage earners in the family

Awareness of Family Members of One Another's Problems

Family members are often unaware of how one another are responding. Frequently, they may be undergoing similar experiences without being able to discuss them or support one another. It is important to identify whether support is being requested but not offered, or is being offered but not accepted. Poor communication may affect the way that needs of family members are expressed and interpreted.

Some parents may feel the need to provide gifts or material possessions for their children to make up for what they feel their children are missing. At the same time children may feel an excessive responsibility to take over for their parents, often in ways that are inappropriate or unwanted. These issues may be potentially destructive or lead to further resentment if they are not brought out into the open.

Family Functioning

Simple parameters of family functioning can be assessed by most therapists. Problems identified that require additional expertise can then be referred to more specialized services. Four areas of family functioning should be assessed: styles and patterns of communication, the ability to recognize and solve problems, the degree and nature of the involvement of family members, and changes or problems in roles.

Communication

Different steps in the process of communication include the ability to (a) express what is being felt, (b) listen to others, (c) negotiate solutions, (d) compromise when differences arise, and (e) evaluate changes being made. Difficulties in these areas will be demonstrated as the family members describe their problems; these difficulties can often be altered by simple interventions aimed at getting family members to talk—and listen—to each other.

Problem Identification and Problem Solving

A large part of a family's success in solving its problems depends on the ability of its members to identify and recognize the true nature of these problems. Dwelling inordinately on a practical problem might, for example, represent an attempt to conceal an underlying marital problem or provide a way to avoid addressing a more affectually loaded or contentious issue.

Family Members' Involvement With One Another

The degree of involvement can be determined by assessing the support family members provide for one another, the amount of expressed criticism, the warmth or distance experienced when family members interact, the extent to which they acknowledge or are affected by one another's distress, and the time they spend together in social activities or in completing family tasks.

Role Changes

The loss of a job can lead to the loss of work roles that may have met or satisfied internal needs, possibly leading to changes in family interactions. It can also mean that family members spend more time together, often in new situations that may require adjustments by all concerned. The family assessment must examine changes that have already been made and those that are still required. The flexibility or rigidity the family demonstrates in making role adjustments should be assessed, as should any external or cultural forces that may be reinforcing maladaptive role behaviors.

For some families the loss of a job can strengthen family relationships. Family members may enjoy the extra time they can spend together, and parents may no longer have to balance competing work and family roles. Some individuals may also take on new roles that are more satisfying, which takes pressure off other parts of the family system. As with individuals, it is important to help families recognize their strengths, resources, and supports.

Stages of Family Development

Each stage of the development and maturation of a family unit involves different tasks and adjustments. These may be fairly straightforward—for example, a couple's response to the arrival or departure of a child—but can be more complex as issues of control or interdependence are resolved. Unemployment can expose or intensify problems that a couple may be struggling with in negotiating a particular stage. For example, members of a family who are struggling with issues of control may not be able to offer each other maximum support during a period of crisis. They may find that their lack of cohesion becomes more of a problem as they try to collaborate to deal with increased external pressures.

Alternatively, the loss of a job can interrupt the natural stages of family growth. An enforced separation of family members as one partner searches for new work or retrains in another community may interfere with attempts by a couple or a young family to become a more integrated or interdependent unit.

Family Activities

It is useful to inquire about what a family does in the time it spends together and whether these activities have been affected by the change in employment status. The time spent together, the nature of the activities, and the quality of the family involvement must all be assessed. It is possible that family members may feel they are spending too much time together. A study of unemployed fathers in Toronto found that initially fathers enjoyed having the additional time to spend with their children (Johnson and Abramovitch 1986). If these fathers found themselves spending too much time with their children, however, they felt that their view of their children became more negative, because the children were seen as a continuing reminder of the changes in life-style or as an impediment to returning to work. In this study affordable day-care was seen as the most needed social service that was not available. Opportunities for getting away from the family, if only for brief periods of time, may be very important.

External Family Supports

A family comes under increasing stress as the period of unemployment lengthens, and emotional resources may become depleted as family members face new situations and additional demands. External support from friends and family may be crucial, and the milieu in which the family exists should be considered. In particular, the availability of practical help—for example, money, child-care, or transportation—should be examined. It is also important to assess whether the family is failing to utilize resources that are available, and if so why.

Material Well-being

Economic deprivation can have a serious impact on a family's ability to cope with joblessness. Finances can easily become the focus of family arguments and disagreements. The assessment should therefore include direct questions on whether the family has reduced savings or increased debts from the year before or has had to cut back on essential items such as food or housing.

Other Wage Earners

The presence of other wage earners who are either working or able to enter the labor force may play a significant role in reducing the amount of economic hardship. This can be a mixed blessing, however, because it can create problems if other family members are reluctant to work, even though they need to do so, or if their working will unbalance family roles and relationships. These issues should be addressed during the assessment.

Social Supports

The third part of the assessment examines an individual's social system, including social activities, social supports, attitudes of social and community contacts, and knowledge of community resources.

Social Activities

It is necessary to look at the types of activities in which an individual participates and whether there have been any changes from preunemployment routines. A simple way of achieving this is to suggest that an hourly diary of activities be kept. This account should include a column that describes and rates the quality of social interactions, which can also provide revealing information on attitudes and perceptions.

Other areas to explore are the cost of social activities, including those that might need to be curtailed if a new job is not forthcoming, and activities the individual is choosing to participate in that might increase social isolation. The establishment of a routine for daily tasks may be extremely helpful in reducing the worker's feeling that the days are amorphous and that time hangs heavily on his or her hands.

Social Support

Information about an individual's network of support can be gathered by asking a few key questions. Who are the main people involved—socially and professionally—and how is their role perceived and their help utilized? Asking these questions requires the therapist to be aware of the functions that are expected of a support network, the ways in which others are informed of the individual's needs and expectations, and the individual's degree of satisfaction with the support that is forthcoming. It is also important to find out what supports—human and organizational—that were previously available through the workplace may need to be replaced.

Attitudes of Social and Community Contacts

An individual's perception of the availability and accessibility of support may differ from the reality, but the perception may be more influential in determining whether supports are utilized. The amount of support provided, however, may not compensate for a lack of quality. If an individual feels that friends and ex-colleagues are critical or patronizing in their responses, he or she may not seek out their help or support or may even find these relationships to be destructive.

It is also important to understand how the individual views unemployment and what he or she perceives the attitude of the local community to be toward the unemployed. In some communities the unemployed may be stigmatized or seen as lazy or worthless. In other communities, especially those used to high levels of unemployment or significant seasonal variations, unemployment may be accepted as part of the way of life. An appreciation of these attitudes can be useful in helping an unemployed individual accept the reality of his or her predicament or take advantage of support that is available.

In many circumstances it may be helpful to include others in the assessment and, if appropriate, in the treatment. As with family interventions, bringing together individuals representing different parts of a support system for a meeting may help to identify and resolve many problems.

Knowledge of Community Resources

Most communities have established a variety of services such as vocational programs, recreation centers, and counseling services that can meet some of the needs of the unemployed. It is worth checking whether the unemployed worker is aware of these programs and knows how to utilize their services, especially if he or she has had no prior reason to do so. Decisions not to use these services may be influenced by embarrassment at requiring such assistance or the need to maintain a sense of independence. Although many services do not meet the needs of all jobless workers, knowing what is available may help.

The Workplace

In some situations it may be important to gather relevant information about the individual's former place of employment. In these cases information should be obtained about the organization or workplace, the work-related support and resources, and the individual's attitudes toward work.

Organization

It is useful to understand the philosophy and management practices of the organization to get some idea of the environment within which the individual used to work and the accuracy of his or her perception as to why the layoff occurred (Levinson 1972). Knowledge of the organization's stage of development, economic health, and market performance can throw light on the reasons why the worker may have lost his or her job and how this might have affected the worker's attitude toward finding another job.

Support and Resources

In many instances workers who have lost their jobs may still be able to take advantage of benefits or resources offered by the employer for a period of time after displacement. The possibility or desirability of maintaining contact with former colleagues should also be assessed, particularly if embarrassment at what has occurred is causing the individual to withdraw from friends or work-related activities.

Attitudes Toward Work

It is worth assessing the effect the loss of the job has had on the individual's attitude toward working, particularly if residual anger is interfering with his or her ability to utilize available supports or find new work. Understanding the nature of the relationships between the organization and its work force may help to explain why certain workers may experience unexpected guilt, remorse, or self-blame at losing their job.

In addition to assessing general attitudes toward working, the therapist should also inquire as to previous periods of unemployment and how these may have come about. Someone who has been fired more than once may develop what Triandis (1975) has referred to as "ecosystem distrust," with a gradual reduction in the individual's trust of authority figures and institutions, which can make it even harder to reintegrate into the work force.

The assessment presented here is comprehensive. Some parts will be appropriate for some individuals, other parts for others. Each area or question that has been highlighted has been included because it can unearth information that can have a bearing on how any individual copes, and provide guidance in developing a management plan.

Many of the areas presented in this assessment are applicable in assessing most work situations. A synopsis of a comprehensive work-related assessment is provided in Table 5-1.

References

Johnson L, Abramovitch R: Between Jobs—Paternal Unemployment and Family Life. Toronto, Social Planning and Rescarch Council, 1986

Levinson H. Organizational Diagnosis. Cambridge, MA, Harvard University Press, 1972

Triandis H: Ecosystem distrust and the hard to employ. J Appl Psychol 60:44–56, 1975

Table 5-1. Outline of areas to cover in a psychiatric work history

Nature of the job	Employer/job title
	Tasks involved
	Stresses (a) within the job
	(b) with peers
	(c) with superiors
	(d) with family life
	Time in position
	Hours worked and shifts
	Opportunities for advancement
	Control over work environment
Job satisfaction	Meets career goals
	Opportunities for using skills
	and interests
	Congruent with self-image
	Material benefits/pension
	Previous thoughts of leaving
	What individual would
	(could) change
	Reinforces/undermines self-image
Work career	Level of education and qualifications
	Previous jobs
	Reason(s) for leaving; duration
	of employment before leaving
	Long-term plans
	Promotions and demotions
	Employment strengths
	and weaknesses
Previous periods of unemployment	Reasons
	Duration
	How ended
	Problems encountered; how solved
	Impact on self/relationships
Attitudes toward work	Attitudes toward working;
	attitudes toward not working
	Spouse's attitude
Work and family	Demands of job on family life
	Demands of working spouse
	Overlap of work activities;
	relative importance
	Support from family

Work and family of origin

Parental jobs and their impact
Parental expectations and interest
Influences on career choice
Reasons for career choice
Thwarted aspirations

Personal factors and work

Authority figures
Autonomy
Dependency
Responsibility
Work habits
Relationship to others;
    expectations of others
Dealing with disappointment
Ability to anticipate and/or
    accommodate change
Power and competition

Psychiatric disorders

Course of illness
Rehabilitation needs
Illness deficits
Work behaviors
Confidence

Work/Job-finding strengths

Skills and aptitudes
Resources
Knowledge of opportunities
Attitude
Contacts

Social activities

Work-linked supports
Employee-linked supports
Time demands; overlap
    among them
Knowledge of community resources

Note. This table is a comprehensive list of areas to pursue when obtaining a psychiatric work history. Although not every question needs to be asked in each case, it is important to cover relevant areas in sufficient depth so that useful information can be elicited. Information can also be obtained on non-occupational aspects of interpersonal or intrapsychic functioning, using work issues as a vehicle that will generate other material.

Chapter 6

What Can Be Done

Chapter 6

What Can Be Done

In order that people may be happy in their work these
three things are needed: They must be fit for it. They
must not do too much of it. And they must have a sense
of success in it.

John Ruskin "Sesame and Lilies"

Although a little simplistic, it is probably fair to say that
the single most effective intervention for the majority of unemployed workers is to obtain another job. Appropriate preparations for this eventuality will figure prominently in most
intervention strategies. Some unemployed individuals will,
however, need additional assistance in many areas of their life,
not only to speed their return to the work force but also to deal
with the impact of the loss of the original job and the consequences of the time spent without work.

Obstacles Faced by Psychiatric Services

Specific interventions, which should be preceded by a comprehensive assessment along the guidelines presented in the previous chapter, can be aimed at the unemployed themselves, their
families, or their social environment. Preventive and educational activities may also need to be considered. When planning such approaches, however, psychiatric services may face
three obstacles that can affect the ways in which problems
present, the kind of services that can be offered, and the interrelationships with other community agencies working with the
unemployed.

127

Reluctance to Utilize Psychiatric Services

Most unemployed workers will not require psychiatric help. Those who do, however, may never have any direct contact with a psychiatric service. In fact they may see the use of such a service as something that is quite alien to their view of themselves and their life-style. These individuals may not recognize the need for psychiatric help or the relevance of psychological solutions to what they consider to be practical problems. They may also be deterred by what they perceive to be the stigma associated with visiting a psychiatrist, although these attitudes appear to be changing. This reluctance is often increased if they do not have insurance coverage and will be faced with a bill for the help they seek. Indeed, when looking for help these individuals are much more likely to contact someone with whom they already have a relationship, such as a family physician, union representative, or church minister.

Limited Role for Traditional Treatments

Traditional psychiatric treatments may be of little value to the majority of individuals who are unemployed. To be optimally effective, psychiatric services need to develop a broad range of clinical options, including prevention and early identification programs, consultation, family assessments, and individual therapy, as well as addressing public policy issues.

Paradoxically, for the private psychiatrist a recognition of the need to employ a wider range of management strategies can create two further problems. Many of the preventive and community interventions require close collaboration between mental health professionals from different disciplines and may not be practical for the private practitioner. Second, unless some form of payment is established to enable psychiatrists to participate in consultative, educational, and preventive programs, the majority of practitioners will be limited to individual and family treatments within their office practice.

Links With Community Agencies

These problems can be overcome if psychiatric services can work closely, collaboratively, and nonobtrusively with representatives of community agencies and others who are in regular contact with the unemployed. Unfortunately, many psychiatric services fail to establish these contacts or appreciate their importance.

Contacts with community agencies and familiarity with their programs can bring an extra dimension to the work of psychiatric services and lead to a wider range of treatment options that may not always involve direct (face-to-face) treatment. When working with these agencies therapists must appreciate the role of indirect clinical activities (those in which the client or patient is not seen but information or support is provided to others working with him or her), and recognize when these activities may constitute a more appropriate intervention.

If these problems can be overcome, psychiatric services are in a unique position to help to reduce the human distress that follows the loss of a job. If a systemic approach such as the one outlined below is followed, the treatment plan that results will be comprehensive and effective.

A Systemic Approach for Psychiatric Services

Psychiatric services can consider five kinds of interventions (Figure 6–1):

- Assessment and treatment of individuals referred to the service for help
- Consultation and support to staff of agencies and other primary caretakers
- Participation in collaborative projects
- Preventive programs in the workplace and the community
- Influencing of social policy

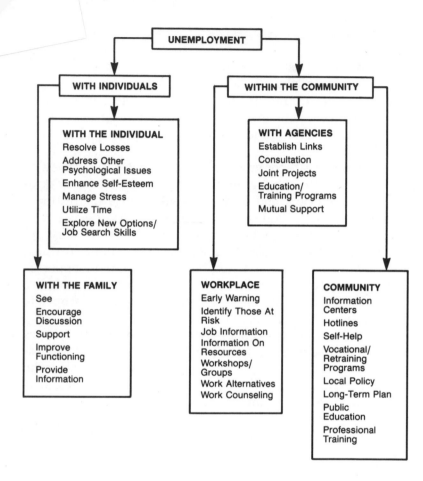

FIGURE 6–1. Intervention strategies with the unemployed.

Treatment

Treatment intervention has two components: (a) treatment of the individual, and (b) interventions with the family. These are usually complementary, and attention needs to be paid to both.

130

The Individual

The therapist who is attempting to help someone who is struggling to cope with the impact of losing a job must address the following important therapeutic tasks.

Dealing with the losses. The capacity to recognize, work through, and come to terms with the losses that follow unemployment may require a slightly different approach than traditional grief work offers. Although each loss may have had a limited impact, the cumulative effect can be magnified, while the losses may continue over a lengthy period of time. The financial deprivation, for example, may necessitate cutbacks or sacrifices many months after the job itself is lost. This prolonged impact creates additional problems for an individual who, while still coming to terms with initial losses, is having to adjust to additional setbacks.

The tasks for the therapist are to help the individual recognize what may have been lost, to provide support in working through the various affectual responses, and to assist the individual to focus on the adjustments he or she may need to make in order to cope. It can be very helpful to put these reactions into a longitudinal time frame and to emphasize that however distressing events may appear to be, their impact will diminish over time. This perspective can also help the maintenance of a sense of continuity and stability, whatever disruptions may be taking place.

Examining unresolved psychological issues. The loss of a job, as with any life crisis, not only creates new challenges but also reawakens unresolved psychological conflicts and dilemmas. Recurring life themes may be aroused by the events connected to the loss of a job. These themes can include difficulties with authority figures, struggles around control or competition, and problems in self-esteem. At this point the therapist may be presented with two opportunities.

The first is to identify relevant psychological themes and

131

the way they may be manifested in an individual's behavior or relationships. This may help the individual understand the strength of his or her reaction, especially if it seems out of proportion to the severity of the event. The second opportunity arises because a period of crisis may be a time when an individual is more receptive to examining underlying issues. He or she may be able to use the therapeutic relationship to make changes that could have a lasting impact, perhaps decreasing the likelihood that events or behaviors that preceded the loss of the job will recur.

Maintaining and increasing self-esteem. Perhaps the single most important therapeutic task is to ensure that blows to self-esteem will be overcome and confidence restored. To achieve this a therapist needs to be nonjudgmental and allow the ventilation of anger or anxiety. These feelings can often be validated simply by the therapist's preparedness to listen and to accept them at face value.

The emphasis is on the preservation of a sense of personal continuity, encouraging the unemployed worker to recognize those things in his or her life that have not changed. Once again, putting present events into a longer-term time frame may be helpful.

Personal strengths should be identified and reinforced. Successes, however small, in any aspect of an individual's life should be pointed out, and situations in which failure may be inevitable should be avoided. For example, applying for jobs where there is little chance of success may lead to a further rejection that could be devastating. The same principle applies to other aspects of treatment. A management plan should be built upon small, attainable targets rather than larger tasks that are less likely to be accomplished, however important they may seem.

Life situations, including the events that led up to the loss of the job, should be reviewed and reappraised. This exercise can demonstrate to individuals how they may have been victims of events beyond their control, while helping to dissipate inappropriate guilt. To offset any feelings of helplessness, individuals should also be encouraged to focus on areas of their life in which they do still have control and can function effectively.

Managing the stress. To cope with the stress of unemployment, treatment should focus on practical issues and emphasize the importance of handling immediate problems, particularly during the initial crisis. Although it is important to address longer-term problems, many of these can be left until the most immediate or pressing issues have been resolved. Problems that may arise can be predicted and strategies for dealing with them worked out.

A realistic approach to finances and budgeting is essential. Unemployed workers should be encouraged to make early adjustments before savings or reserve resources are depleted. If unable to do so, they should also be dissuaded from trying to maintain their previous life-style simply to try to keep up appearances or pretend that nothing has happened. Stress management and relaxation skills can also be taught, often in a group where individuals can benefit from the support and understanding of others going through similar experiences.

Utilizing time productively. Productive time utilization by the unemployed individual often depends on the establishment of a routine or timetable so that each day is not spent just waiting for the hours to pass. The unemployed individual should be encouraged to set up a routine as quickly as possible. Efforts also need to be made to maintain the continuity of relationships, activities, and memberships, something the therapist may need to facilitate by inviting others to participate in sessions.

One possible participatory activity involves working as a volunteer, but this option may have mixed benefits. On the one hand, volunteering can compensate for many of the things the job had provided, such as companionship and a sense of achievement. On the other hand, working without remuneration will not help an individual's financial situation and may accentuate the difference between him or her and those who are paid to work.

Exploring new possibilities. Every encouragement should be provided to help an individual find a new job. Job skills and options and long-term career plans should be reappraised before the individual embarks on a job search. This is one area in which it is essential for psychiatric services to have established links with specialized community agencies that offer work programs.

The search for a new job should be taken as seriously as working itself, with sufficient time and energy being devoted to the task. The therapist can offer simple tips such as how to put together a presentable resume, how to prepare a personal information sheet that can be referred to when filling in job application forms, and how to build and take advantage of support networks and contacts, as many jobs are found by personal tips or word of mouth. Workers may also find it helpful to read about the experiences of others who have coped with a period of unemployment recounted in books such as *What Color Is Your Parachute?* (Bolles 1978).

It may also be a time to look at different career opportunities. For some workers a review of skills and abilities may help them recognize that many of these skills are transferable and will stand them in good stead in a new career. Other displaced workers may see unemployment as presenting a window of opportunity but may require support and encouragement to take a chance and do something different. In these cases, the loss of a job may in the long run prove to be liberating.

Other Situations in Individual Treatment

The therapist can encounter other clinical situations such as those that involve workers who experience a severe crisis at the time of losing their job, workers or their relatives who develop severe psychiatric symptomatology during a period of unemployment, or long-term psychiatric patients who may face additional obstacles when entering the work force due to their illness. These situations may require different approaches.

Crises. In crisis situations, the sudden loss of a job can lead to numerous problems in quick succession, particularly if there had been little advance warning. The sense of rejection can create feelings of worthlessness, while the loss of social contacts or of a routine can deprive an individual of support at a time he or she most needs it. Feelings of guilt, shame, anger, and anxiety can be overwhelming. The main focus in these situations should be on maintaining a sense of personal continuity, dealing with immediate problems, mobilizing family and social supports, and practical problem solving.

Severe symptoms. The combined effects of the losses, stress, changes in self-esteem, and reduced support can produce severe psychological symptoms. These are most likely to present as depression or anxiety and may arise many months or even years after the job has been lost. The therapist must ensure that the individual receives appropriate treatment, especially if the initial presentation is to a family physician or a community agency. If the symptoms are severe enough to interfere with day-to-day activities, they may need to be treated energetically before the individual can participate productively in other kinds of therapies or programs.

Long-term psychiatric patients. The problems of unemployment are particularly acute for the chronically mentally disabled, who may already have deficits that affect their participation in the work force. Many of the simple entry jobs that could help lower-functioning individuals return to the work force or rebuild their confidence have disappeared or are now being filled by more highly qualified workers. The workplace may be less tolerant of those who are disabled, while repeated setbacks can lower an individual's confidence or decrease his or her motivation to try to find a job. Even sheltered workshops, which used to provide a "protected" work environment, are becoming more competitive, taking on increasingly demanding work tasks and expecting a higher level of performance from participants.

An appreciation of the importance of working highlights the central role of work in psychiatric rehabilitation and the need for appropriate vocational programs, geared to an individual's current level of functioning. Ideally, communities should establish a sequential range of programs, each aimed at individuals with similar degrees of severity of deficits or levels of functioning. In this approach a participant can move from one level to another as his or her skills increase and confidence builds.

Vocational programs should begin with a comprehensive assessment of skills, abilities, and interests before a plan is worked out or a placement considered. Wherever possible, these programs should offer realistic work experiences in natural work settings, providing reasonable remuneration for work that is being performed. Ongoing support, education, and training in work tasks and work behaviors should be integral parts of vocational rehabilitation activities. Situations that limit or undermine an individual's creativity, self-respect, or image of himself or herself as a worthwhile productive citizen should be avoided.

The Family

In addition to examining the family's perceptions of what has taken place and the effect their responses may be having on the person who is jobless, it is always necessary to remember the impact unemployment might be having on other family members. The most important intervention may be to meet with the entire family to initiate a discussion of topics the family may have had difficulty addressing by themselves. All family members should be encouraged to participate, and each should be given a chance to describe his or her fears and hopes. Simply expressing these emotions and hearing the response of other family members can lead to a realization that the family share many common feelings and reactions; it also can provide an opportunity to be sad or angry, reduce guilt, and help the family cope better as a unit. In fact coping with the stress of the loss of a job can often help a family pull together and become closer.

The family should be helped to establish clear patterns of communication. The therapist can help family members listen to one another, checking to make sure they understand what they are hearing. This is an essential step toward helping the family recognize and resolve problems. It is worthwhile asking each member to describe the problems he or she sees the family facing. Common issues raised or discrepancies between the views of different family members can be identified. The therapist should try to differentiate between preexisting problems that predated or were exacerbated by the job loss and problems stemming from the loss of the job, although all need to be addressed.

Necessary role adjustments can be identified—usually in behavioral terms—and new roles negotiated, practiced, and reinforced. Successful adjustments the family has already made or successes in other areas should be acknowledged. Cultural assumptions that may be affecting the family's adjustment to change may need to be challenged gently.

Families also benefit from receiving information on vocational or recreational resources and should be encouraged to utilize available supports even though they might be embarrassed about the implications of what has taken place. Explaining the problems that the family may face over time and discussing the ways they might handle these problems are also important.

Psychiatric Consultation and Backup

Although a small number of unemployed workers will eventually come into contact with mental health services, most of the problems of the unemployed are not of sufficient severity to warrant ongoing psychiatric treatment. Many jobless people may see little personal relevance in psychiatric care, preferring to work with staff of agencies they have already contacted and with whom psychiatric services may have limited connections.

Interrelationships between the different levels of services can be conceptualized in the form of a pyramid (Figure 6–2). When facing a personal problem or life crisis, an individual is most likely to turn to immediate informal supports such as friends, neighbors, and family members. This individual is then likely to contact more formal community supports with whom a relationship has already been established—for example, his or her family physician or church minister. The third level of service may be a community agency that helps with practical day-to-day problems such as work, housing, or welfare. Finally, when symptoms become more severe or problems become harder to contain, the individual may contact more specialized health or mental health services.

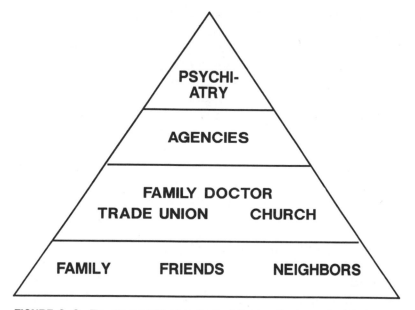

FIGURE 6–2. The "pyramid" of contacts following the loss of a job.

To be able to respond to the different ways in which the psychological problems of the unemployed may present, psychiatric services must be able to offer more than just ongoing direct care. They must also offer consultative services, psychiatric backup, and other indirect services where the focus may be on improving the skills of the community caretakers rather than treating an identified patient. Such services can be targeted at the agencies or programs that have the maximum contact with unemployed people in distress or that have contracted to work with groups of unemployed workers to facilitate their reentry into the labor market.

One mechanism for achieving this extended role of psychiatric services is through the establishment of consultation relationships between key community agencies and psychiatrists or mental health services. In this arrangement the consultant visits the agency for a regular period of time—a half a day a month, for example—to review and discuss cases and problems the agency is handling. Once the basis of the relationship has been established, it can be expanded to include telephone advice in between visits as well as direct interventions with clients of the agency during a consultation visit, if appropriate.

Staff of community agencies often feel more comfortable working with more severely distressed unemployed individuals if they know that support is available should the problems exceed their capabilities. In addition, their clients may receive the benefit of the advice of a specialist without feeling any stigma at being referred to psychiatry. Approaches to cases discussed can also often be generalized by agency staff to other cases with whom they are working.

The same principle applies when working with family physicians. Family physicians will have contact with most unemployed people over the duration of their time out of work, but may not recognize the problems they are seeing or know how to manage these problems when they are identified. Most family physicians could benefit from information on how to recognize the problems associated with job loss, the interventions they can employ in their office practices, and the availability of local resources. One way of achieving this is through specially prepared educational kits on problems and local resources that can be distributed to all family physicians within a community.

Collaborative Activities With Community Agencies

Many community agencies provide services for the unemployed and their families. Although their clients may not be severely impaired or disabled by psychological symptoms, there are many ways in which these agencies could benefit from greater collaboration with psychiatric services. These activities can be divided into two categories: (a) contributions to educational and training programs, and (b) participation in joint projects and providing mutual support.

Educational and Training Programs

Psychiatric services can help staff of community agencies improve their skills in recognizing and handling the problems of the unemployed people they encounter. Such programs should be relevant to the needs, background, and clientele of each individual agency. The goals of these programs should be to assist agency staff to recognize the ways in which the emotional problems that follow job loss may present and to identify those unemployed individuals who may be at higher risk of developing more severe emotional problems.

It is important to provide agency staff with a framework for understanding how unemployment and its effects may be transmitted, and how these effects change over time. They should also be informed about available psychiatric services and how they can refer their clients to these services. In all cases, staff should be trained in a problem-based, rather than a diagnosis-focused, approach. Agency staff should concentrate on identifying problems and assessing their severity rather than worrying whether the individuals they are seeing meet the criteria for a major psychiatric disorder.

Mental health services should view their work with community agencies as part of a two-way relationship. Agency staff have a different perspective and can provide a more realistic picture of the predicament of the individuals they are seeing on a daily basis. If psychiatric consultants allow themselves to learn from these contacts, they can broaden their own appreciation of the impact of job loss and have a better understanding of the context in which emotional problems can develop. A consultant who respects the work of other professionals and recognizes the limits of his or her own expertise is much more likely to be welcomed and be able to work effectively. This awareness also makes it less likely that consultants will end up "medicalizing" work-related problems, defining them in psychiatric terms so that they fit a more limited frame of reference or understanding of the problem.

Joint Programs and Mutual Support

The frustrations of dealing with problems to which there are no simple answers or which create multiple difficulties can be draining and disconcerting for caretakers as well as for the unemployed themselves. Interagency contacts and cooperation can help staff of different services provide each other with much needed support and encouragement, as well as offering a forum for an exchange of ideas about solutions to common problems.

These contacts can also stimulate the development of collaborative programs in which several agencies contribute resources and expertise. One example might be a crisis line, run by volunteers who may be trained or backed up by staff of mental health services. Another would be information workshops in the workplace, presented by representatives of different agencies and whose purpose is to offer comprehensive educational programs for workers about to be displaced.

Agencies should also collaborate to compile statistics on the problems they are seeing to chronicle the impact of unemployment and to support submissions for new programs.

Preventive Interventions

Preventive interventions are feasible in situations where there is advance warning, or a clear indication, of the possibility of an imminent layoff or plant closure. The nature and speed of any response will depend on many specific local factors. These include the size of the community, the impact of the plant on a community's social and economic functioning, the attitude of the employer and the work force, financial resources, local leadership, and political will.

A variety of preventive interventions are discussed in the following pages. Not all will be applicable for each particular situation. From this array of options each community needs to choose those programs that best suit or can best be adapted to the local context. The greater the degree of local input in designing flexible programs that reflect the characteristics and needs of a particular community or workplace, the greater the chance of success. This was demonstrated by Cook (1987) in a review of early intervention programs in nine different plants across the United States. In each case, the more the program planners could take local geography, demography, traditions, and culture into consideration, the more successful the reemployment outcomes were for participants.

Preventive interventions can be divided into those that predate the loss of jobs (interventions that can be directed at the workplace or the community), and those that are initiated after the jobs are lost (interventions that usually take place within the community).

The goal of workplace interventions is to help workers understand their predicament, regain a sense of control, learn about material and support resources that are available, and make adequate preparations for future eventualities (Stone and Kieffer 1984). Underlying this are the goals of strengthening the role of the workplace as a focus for these efforts and of building upon strengths and resources that already exist. These interventions are much more likely to succeed if labor and management can collaborate to solve common problems.

142

Community-directed preventive programs attempt to enhance the capacity of the local environment to offer support and practical help to enable workers and their families to survive, cope, and find alternative employment. They also try to raise the awareness of the ways in which unemployment affects individuals and communities and of how communities can contribute to the generation or amelioration of stress.

Interventions Within the Workplace

There is evidence that interventions within the workplace prior to job loss can prevent some of the immediate sequelae of unemployment, but many workers fail to take advantage of such programs (Cook 1987; Gordus et al. 1981). Those workers who do so may be those who would be more likely to make preparations or take the impending job loss more seriously regardless. Workplace interventions apply mainly to situations in which there is to be a major layoff or plant closure, rather than to cases in which individual workers lose their jobs or are fired.

Interventions within the workplace mean that potentially all affected workers can be reached. Problems can then be dealt with before they become disruptive. These interventions also provide a chance to identify workers who may require additional training or assistance to cope, who may be failing to make appropriate preparations, or who are at risk of developing more serious problems.

The first, and perhaps the most crucial, intervention is to provide workers with as much forewarning of layoffs and redundancies as possible in order to give them the opportunity to make any necessary preparations. The provision of practical information is essential. This can be achieved through the dissemination of written materials and resource guides, one-to-one interviews with affected workers, and educational workshops or seminars.

Written materials should be easy to read and should contain relevant practical information on worker entitlements and how to apply for benefits, free recreation activities for workers

143

and their families, training and retraining opportunities, and possible problems that may be faced. These materials can also provide information on community resources that might be helpful when dealing with potential problems. These resources might include financial and budgeting services, legal services, accommodation, counseling programs, health services, leisure and recreation services, and activities for all family members.

Educational workshops, with contributions from staff of different agencies and services, can also be an effective means of communicating this information. The content can focus on coping and dealing with the emotional and interpersonal aspects of losing a job or on the practical aspects of finding new work. In the former, the problems likely to be encountered can be reviewed, and the preparations that workers can make to prevent these problems from happening can be discussed. Specific coping skills such as problem solving or stress management can also be taught. If relevant to participants, a workshop might choose to concentrate on a more specific issue such as coping with early retirement.

Helping workers cope with the emotional responses generated by job loss can often best be handled in a group setting, although this may be seen by many workers as having little personal relevance. A group run by someone who is not connected to the workplace may provide workers with more of an opportunity to vent their feelings and prepare themselves for what may come.

Workshops on finding alternative work should cover ways of looking for a new job and the utilization of vocational services. Job search information can include the local availability of work alternatives, retraining programs or relocation schemes, ways of looking for new jobs, techniques for appraising skills, and the intake criteria of community agencies that help with specific work-related problems.

The workplace should also support efforts by workers to find new jobs and ensure that they have sufficient flexibility within their workday to look for other jobs or attend interviews. One way of achieving this is through the utilization of employee assistance programs (American Psychiatric Association 1989). Another option is the establishment of an employer- or employer/union-sponsored job counseling or out-placement program, whereby outside agencies attempt to help displaced workers find alternative employment. More private companies are now contracting to offer this service. Evidence from such programs across the United States stresses the need for flexibility in these initiatives. There is no one specific model or approach to be followed in every setting. Each community or workplace should develop programs that fit the needs of its workers and the local job situation. Further evaluation of these programs needs to take place to assess their efficacy as well as the implications of different forms of sponsorship (government, management, labor, private agencies, or through a collaborative effort).

For therapists or mental health services considering workplace interventions, the first decision to make is the extent to which they will be active participants in these activities. In many situations, the initiation or organization of such programs lies beyond the skills or resources of mental health services. The most useful contribution of these services may be to establish links with community services that are more centrally involved or are prime movers in organizing the programs. Mental health service staff can then be incorporated into programs when appropriate, bringing a different perspective to understanding the problems of coping with unemployment. They can also provide clinical or consultative backup to agencies more directly involved in the workplace.

Interventions Within the Community

Community interventions can take place at a number of levels. Some interventions reflect the efforts of informal groups such as unemployed workers or churches, while others are organized more formally by community agencies or government. Agencies, either individually or collectively, can publicize the predicament of the unemployed and attempt to influence gov-

145

erning bodies, especially at the local or municipal level, to adopt policies that will ease the burdens of the unemployed.

Many of the principles already discussed apply here. Every effort should be made to ensure that workers are provided with all available information. Programs are more effective if agencies and services with different mandates and perspectives can share their expertise and resources.

Some communities have established information centers or clearinghouses that offer practical advice, counseling, support, and information for the unemployed. Many communities have also established emergency hotlines or crisis centers, often staffed by individuals who themselves have been unemployed and are trained and backed up by mental health workers.

These services are often set up at times of rapid increases in unemployment rates, but unfortunately they only receive temporary funding. Initial funding may not be renewed, especially if unemployment rates appear to be falling or the public perception is that unemployment is a less serious problem. There are numerous examples of effective programs that have been forced to close because of a lack of ongoing funding once their start-up money runs out, irrespective of need.

Self-help or mutual support groups for unemployed workers can serve many functions, providing support, solidarity, a sense of purpose, and information for their members. However, they need not only serve a support function. Job clubs, for example, enable unemployed workers to gather regularly to share information and leads on jobs that may be available. Such initiatives need to be actively supported by social agencies and organized labor.

One problem commonly encountered by self-help organizations is maintaining their longer-term stability. The membership and leadership frequently change as participants return to the work force, leading to a loss of continuity or lack of direction within the group. Self-help groups may have a greater chance of enduring if they have a more specific focus, such as groups formed by disabled workers.

146

Communities should be able to offer a comprehensive range of vocational and retraining programs. Job creation schemes are valuable but should lead to real work and continuing jobs rather than simply serving the function of making unemployment statistics appear better. The impact of multiple dislocations—the loss of the original job followed by the loss of the training program job—can sometimes be more destructive than a continuing period of unemployment, especially if the participant was led to believe that retraining would lead to permanent work.

It may also be possible to persuade municipal governments to adopt policies such as reduced bus fares or cheaper admission to recreational or cultural activities. Although there is a danger that these policies may intensify a sense of dependency on the part of unemployed workers or reinforce the stigma of being different, they can increase the workers' participation within the community and reduce the stress faced.

Communities must also attempt to predict future economic changes and develop long-term employment and job diversification strategies, especially if they are faced with the potential closure of their single industry or the departure of a major employer. Advance planning improves the likelihood of success in adjusting to such a situation.

Public Education and Professional Training

Psychiatric services must not forget that the psychological effects of job loss develop within a wider social and political context. Many interventions are unlikely to have any lasting impact unless wider social inequities that render particular individuals or groups more vulnerable are corrected and social conditions that can exaggerate the stress that follows job loss are improved.

In particular, psychiatric services have an obligation to ensure that the human dimension remains an integral part of a public debate that all too often focuses on impersonal statistics or poorly substantiated societal priorities. There is no single solution to the complex problems unemployment creates—or that create unemployment—but the human cost and the destructiveness of being without work should be central when these issues are being discussed.

Of equal importance in the long run is the need to address the implications for all workers—employed or otherwise—of the adjustments that societies will have to make to accommodate the changing nature of work. Psychiatry's understanding of the meaning of work and work's interrelationship with family and social activities places psychiatry in an ideal situation to educate and intervene in these areas.

There are also ways in which mental health workers can bring about changes in their own community, including public education. (See Chapter 8 for discussion of wider policy issues.) This process may involve speaking at public meetings, participating in community seminars and local educational activities, and raising unemployment-related issues during media appearances. Mental health professionals may find other agencies or organizations receptive to suggestions that they be included in public forums on work-related issues.

Educational programs on the impact of unemployment can be aimed at all community groups. Priority should be given to programs aimed at those responsible for assisting the unemployed in the community, at workers at higher risk of losing their jobs, and at teenagers who are still at school. Young people, especially those with lower educational qualifications, need to prepare themselves appropriately prior to entering the work force.

The impact of work and job loss must also figure in the training of all health workers. The training that psychiatrists receive rarely equips them to deal with the problems that unemployment presents. Psychiatry residents need to learn how to take a comprehensive occupational history and interpret the information they have elicited. They should learn to work with community agencies, understanding and respecting their respective roles, and should be comfortable working as consultants in locations other than their offices. They also must recognize the interrelationships of work, family, and social activities and how these can lead to different interventions.

Mental health services can participate actively in the development of innovative programs for groups of unemployed workers and alternate work strategies, such as job sharing, that could lead to the creation of new jobs. They must also ensure that accurate statistics detailing the impact of unemployment are collected and intervention programs evaluated so that contributions to discussions of public policy are based on scientific data in addition to anecdotal evidence and a sense of social justice.

As unemployment levels fall and the issue begins to recede in the minds of those who control funding or set public policy, these kinds of educational initiatives become even more important. As more of the unemployed become "hard-core" (i.e., out of work for more than a year), the need to avoid divisions between those who are working and those who are not and to decrease the sense of alienation of the unemployed becomes crucial.

References

American Psychiatric Association, Committee on Occupational Psychiatry: Employee assistance programs and the role of the psychiatrist: report of the Committee on Occupational Therapy. Am J Psychiatry 146:690–694, 1989

Bolles RN: What Color Is Your Parachute? Berkeley, CA, Ten Speed Press, 1978

Cook R: Worker Dislocations: Case Studies of Causes and Cures. Kalamazoo, MI, WE Upjohn Institute for Employment Research, 1987

Gordus JP, Jarley P, Ferman L: Plant Closings and Economic Dislocation. Kalamazoo, MI, WE Upjohn Institute for Employment Research, 1981

Stone J, Kieffer C: Pre-Layoff Intervention: A Response to Unemployment. Ann Arbor, MI, Institute of Science and Technology, University of Michigan, 1984

Chapter 7

Coping With Unemployment: Case Examples

Chapter 7

Coping With Unemployment: Case Examples

He only earns his freedom and existence who daily con-
quers them anew.

Goethe "Court of the Palace"

*T*he cases outlined in this chapter illustrate ways in which
the problems associated with unemployment may present.[1]
They also demonstrate the application of the model described
in Chapter 4 and ways in which it leads to specific intervention
strategies.

The Committed Worker

Mr. Simpson was a 47-year-old single man, referred for psychiatric follow-up after a 3-week admission following a suicide attempt. This attempt had occurred 2 weeks after he was laid off
from the job he had held for 25 years.

Mr. Simpson had experienced an impoverished childhood, spending many of his early years in foster homes in a
poor rural community. As a teenager he had moved to a larger
community to find work and had been working as a tool-and-
die maker ever since. He was a man of limited self-confidence
and interpersonal skills and had few social contacts outside of

---

[1] The names of all individuals involved have been changed in the following
examples.

work. He spent much of his leisure time helping out with paperwork at his local trade union headquarters. His main recreational activity was gardening, and his immediate reaction upon losing his job was to assume he would be unable to meet his mortgage payments and would have to sell his home and lose his garden. Unable to cope with the potential losses, he attempted to take his own life.

Impressions

Mr. Simpson was extremely invested in his job, which compensated for many of the deficiencies in other aspects of his life. The loss of the job led to a sudden sense of isolation or anomie, accentuated by the absence of social support. The prospect of having to give up his garden, his most valued possession, led to a sense of hopelessness, and these factors precipitated the suicide attempt.

Interventions

Mr. Simpson responded well to the support of his therapist. His first task was to draw up a realistic budget, which helped him realize that he would be able to afford to keep his house. One important social support was identified: a family from a neighboring town whom he had avoided calling because of his embarrassment at having been laid off. The family members were invited to a session, where their support was apparent, and they immediately invited him to spend a weekend with them, an offer he was delighted to accept.

Mr. Simpson was encouraged to work as a volunteer to rebuild his confidence until he could find further work; this gave him a sense of being needed. His union agreed to allow him to continue to help out with office tasks, and he began his job search. After 6 months, Mr. Simpson had found new and equivalent work and was discharged from psychiatric care, feeling as well as he had felt in the previous 5 years. He decided to continue with his volunteering even after returning to work. In this case resolution of the problems related to unemployment resulted in life-style changes with long-term personal benefits.

The Immigrant

Mr. Wilson was a 45-year-old married father of three who emigrated from Iran in 1979, following the Islamic Revolution. He had previously held a middle management job in the hotel trade while his wife worked in a laboratory in a more prestigious position.

He found work fairly quickly in the community where his wife's family had settled previously, and held the same job as a machinist for 8 years until the plant closed. At work he remained relatively isolated and was the butt of his colleagues' jokes about his homeland. Nine months after plant closure Mr. Wilson was one of only 8% of the work force who remained unemployed. Because of symptoms of depression that appeared to be inhibiting his job search, he was referred for a psychiatric assessment by a counseling service assigned to work with the displaced workers.

The initial assessment revealed no clinical evidence of depression, but Mr. Wilson was unrealistic about finding new work and uncomfortable that his wife's family had secure, well-paying jobs while he remained unemployed. The biggest problem he identified was with his marriage. His wife had not worked since leaving Iran, and he found her increasingly unsupportive and demanding. He felt that she did not understand his predicament, and the fact that she had put on weight and did not look like an "American woman" made him reluctant to be seen with her at social events.

Impressions

Three major factors were complicating Mr. Wilson's adjustment. The first was a long-standing problem with self-esteem, reflected in his feelings of inferiority when compared to his relatives and his need to inflate his own sense of importance while undermining his wife's.

The second problem was an exacerbation of preexisting marital problems. Mr. Wilson's attempts to compensate for a loss of respect as a worker had led to him becoming more domineering and less empathetic with his wife, whose response had been to withdraw from him even more. His traditional view of the role of a husband had made him reluctant to take on additional tasks at home, interpreting these as excessive demands by a nagging wife.

Third, while the husband and wife were unable to support each other, neither had well-developed external support systems. Mr. Wilson had lost the few social contacts he had developed at work and was looking for something to do, while being aware of the limitations imposed by their financial situation. His wife, who spoke very limited English, had family support but little opportunity to do anything outside the family home.

Interventions

Mr. Wilson was only seen once. He canceled a follow-up interview arranged for himself and his wife, stating that he was feeling better and did not need further help. Attempts to review social activities met with little success. He was linked with an employment agency, through the workplace, and continued to attend regularly, although with little progress.

The Wife

Kelly Radford, a 28-year-old homemaker, was referred by her family physician for a psychiatric consultation because of recent symptoms of depression and anxiety. Early in the consultation she mentioned that 6 months previously her husband had been laid off from his laboring job with a small local company, and since that time she had not been able to cope with the changes in his behavior.

He had become more argumentative and much less attentive to her and the children, spending longer periods of time with his friends away from home, and his drinking had increased. He was no longer taking care of the monthly bills or financial commitments for which his wife had had to take over responsibility. Mrs. Radford had not previously experienced any psychiatric problems but felt there had always been difficulties within the marriage. She was now having trouble managing her children and coping with day-to-day household tasks, and she was feeling badly about her inability to manage.

Impressions

Mr. Radford was having difficulty coping with the embarrassment that followed the loss of his job. Some of his anger at being laid off was directed at his family, exposing preexisting marital problems in communication and role definitions while alienating himself from an important source of support. He had responded to these pressures by avoiding many of his family responsibilities.

Mrs. Radford, who described herself as having long-standing problems with self-confidence, was faced with increased responsibilities in many areas of her life. At the same time, she was receiving less support from her husband and was increasingly uncertain about their future because her husband was finding little success in his half-hearted attempts to find work. These difficulties were magnified by the family's problems in meeting their financial obligations.

Interventions

Because Mr. Radford initially refused to attend a conjoint session, the focus of treatment with Mrs. Radford was to help her to see that her "symptoms" reflected her situation rather than an illness and to identify areas in which she was coping well, particularly as a parent. She was also linked with a stress management group and informed of local programs that would give her a break from the children during the day.

Eventually a home visit was conducted in an effort to engage her husband. After some initial hesitancy he talked of his personal reactions since losing his job. He agreed to meet with the therapist for two further sessions that examined his anger and shame at losing his job and probed his knowledge of available community resources. This led to a more energetic and skillful job search that was quickly successful. These sessions were reinforced by marital therapy, which helped the couple make role adjustments, improve their communication, and resolve some of their immediate problems. One session included their two children, who were able to tell their father how much they wanted their "old daddy back." This appeared to have an immediate and lasting effect on him, and after 9 months the family was discharged, with Mr. and Mrs. Radford feeling that they were getting along as well as at any time during their marriage.

The Older Worker

Mr. McLintock was a 57-year-old married man referred by his family physician for treatment of depression, anxiety, and many nonspecific physical symptoms of one year's duration. These symptoms had begun approximately 6 months after he had been laid off from his job as a construction worker.

His wife had suggested that he see his family physician because she had become concerned and frustrated with his social withdrawal, poor mood, and lack of enthusiasm with no obvious precipitants. There was no history of any previous psychiatric problems, and Mrs. McLintock described the premorbid marital relationship as warm and supportive.

Mr. McLintock presented as clinically depressed. He had enjoyed his work but saw little likelihood of ever being employed again because of his physical symptoms, which he blamed for much of his current predicament. He described himself as worthless and expressed little interest in activities he had previously enjoyed. He recognized the changes in his marriage but felt there was nothing he could do to alter this course.

Impressions

While he had been working, Mr. McLintock's identity had been reinforced by his ability to provide, and he had been a reliable and respected worker. Losing his job had been a major blow to which he still had not adjusted, and attempts to find new work had not been successful partly because he was competing against younger, healthier workers.

These unsuccessful attempts to find work had reinforced a sense of shame and worthlessness, which had led, in turn, to increased feelings of depression and social withdrawal. The physical symptoms had become a face-saving explanation of why he was unable to find work. Mr. McLintock found it difficult, however, to recognize a connection between his emotional problems and his reaction to losing his job.

Interventions

Initially, no attempt was made to persuade Mr. McLintock that his symptoms were not physical in origin. A course of antidepressant medication was instituted, and he was seen on a regular basis partly to inquire as to the progress of his "illness" but also to discuss activities in which he might be interested in participating if he were to feel better.

Over a 3-month period his mood improved and his symptoms lessened, although never to the point at which he felt he was able to return to work. He was able to reestablish social contacts, and he expanded the scope of his activities with his wife, including a cross-country car trip to see his children.

By 6 months there had been further improvement, but the McLintock's had resigned themselves to the fact that Mr. McLintock would not work again. His wife had decided to take an early retirement so that the couple could travel together. Their care was transferred back to the family physician, who assumed the role of overseeing the couple's continuing social readjustment.

The Younger Worker

George McNab was a 20-year-old single male, living with his parents, who was referred for an assessment of depressed mood by his family physician at the suggestion of his mother. From the outset it was apparent that he was attending the session unwillingly, mainly because of pressure from his parents, and saw little reason for a psychiatric assessment.

George had been a poor student, which perplexed and exasperated his parents, both of whom had high academic expectations of their children (expectations that George's older brother and sister had been able to meet). George had left school at 16 and had held a variety of service jobs for brief periods of time, each of which he had left because he felt that he was not being paid enough or that the job was going nowhere. He disliked living at home and resented his parents' interference but felt he could not afford to move out.

His depression appeared to be caused primarily by frustration and dissatisfaction with his living situation, but his resentment toward authority figures seemed to prevent him from wishing to discuss these issues with the therapist.

Impressions

George was in the middle of an adolescent identity struggle that had not been helped by his inability to establish himself as an independent and productive adult. This struggle for identity came on top of long-standing family problems and high expectations from unintentionally critical parents. Their criticism reinforced his low self-esteem and accentuated his dilemma in wanting to separate from his family without feeling confident enough, or ready, to do so.

Interventions

It was obvious that George was unlikely to engage in individual treatment, but he did agree to a single, lengthy family session. Both parents were responsive to their son's requests and were able to see how they might be making his transition to greater independence harder. Although they found it difficult to accept their son's lack of aptitude for an academic career, they agreed to support his efforts in entering a government-sponsored training program for young unemployed people.

A variety of other changes in behavior connected to their son's participation in this program and aimed at increasing George's sense of independence were negotiated. Despite the progress made in this session, George refused to return for any follow-up, which was accepted as being a decision he had made for himself. The family agreed to follow up with their family physician with whom they had a good relationship and who was fully briefed about the problems and plans. At 6 months George was still attending his training program, where he had demonstrated a previously unsuspected mechanical aptitude, and was saving to move into his own apartment.

The Executive

Mr. Robert Rice, 45 years old, was referred for a psychiatric assessment by his family physician, who was concerned about his patient's increasing drinking and social deterioration over a 6-month period. Mr. Rice had been laid off from an executive position with a large corporation that he had held for 8 years, during an office realignment 2 years prior to the referral. Since that time he had been unable to hold a job for more than a few weeks, complaining that the jobs he found were demeaning and did not offer the same responsibilities or opportunities as his previous employment.

During the same period, his wife and three children had left him, and he was faced with substantial monthly support payments that necessitated his moving into a smaller apartment, although he retained a country cottage for his personal use. He had been involved in numerous casual but unsatisfying relationships with women, his drinking had increased, and he had alienated most of his former friends and colleagues.

At an initial assessment interview, it became apparent that many of these problems predated the loss of the job. Mr. Rice had been a high flyer early in his career, with his wife grudgingly accepting the need for him to work lengthy hours as he attempted to further his career. Although his performance had started to slip prior to his dismissal, he perceived his firing as having been unfair and felt there was someone in the company who was envious of his achievements. Despite his mild symptoms of depression, the primary problem appeared to relate to his dependent and narcissistic personality traits.

Impressions

Mr. Rice had encountered problems in interpersonal relationships for most of his adult life, looking for others to take care of him and meet his needs but becoming angry and blaming his environment if this did not happen. Underlying these problems was a sense of inadequacy and a lack of self-confidence. His work had become increasingly important to him as one of the few areas of success in his life. This led him to put in longer hours to the exclusion of most other relationships, including his relationship with his wife, whose demands he felt were excessive. He continued to entertain nagging doubts about his ability to perform his job at the level to which he had risen, and even before being laid off, the small mistakes he had made had undermined his self-confidence and led to an increase in his drinking.

Mr. Rice's lack of insight into his problems led him to deny the real reasons for the loss of his job. The blame for this, and for further failures, was externalized, with little attempt being made to take personal responsibility for what was happening. The break-up of his marriage and the ensuing loss of support may have been inevitable but was hastened by his egocentric and demanding behavior once unemployed. The increased financial pressures led to heavy borrowing to try to maintain a life-style that would perpetuate an image of himself as a social success, but as the problems mounted and he failed to find what he was searching for, he became angrier, drank more heavily, and blamed the world for his predicament.

Interventions

Attempts were made to engage Mr. Rice in supportive therapy with the focus being on identifying the problems he faced and coming to terms with the reality of his situation. Counseling for his alcoholism was also recommended. Mr. Rice returned for a follow-up appointment but became angry when the treatment plan was discussed. He refused to come back for any further sessions, and when his family physician tried to follow through with a similar approach, Mr. Rice stopped visiting him as well.

The Psychiatrically Disabled

Barnett Storey, a 26-year-old single male living at home with his parents, had a 9-year history of schizophrenia with six previous hospital admissions, the most recent lasting for 8 months. Because of the deficits of his illness, his limited social skills, and his lack of confidence, he had never been able to work—even in a sheltered work setting—or to live apart from his family.

He was attending a community mental health center regularly, where he received medication and support, but he had been reluctant to participate in other community rehabilitation programs or group activities at the center that had been recommended. He presented as depressed, despondent, and devoid of any belief in his own strengths or abilities. His family was well meaning but was frequently critical of his lack of progress, and Barnie could not name anyone other than his therapist with whom he felt he had a supportive relationship.

Impressions

Not having worked since leaving school because of his illness, Barnie had not had the opportunity to internalize an image of himself as a competent worker or to discover skills he might possess. His depression, stemming from his lack of success in any aspect of his life, contributed to his hopelessness for the future. He had avoided rehabilitation programs because of a fear of failure, which he also perceived as letting down his parents. He was also scared of the intensity of the interpersonal relationships that might develop when working in the same room as other workers.

Interventions

In collaboration with his therapist a very limited work program was developed that allowed for the anxiety Barnie experienced in such situations. This program involved him participating in a half-day work program at the center twice a week, where he performed simple assembly tasks for which he was paid, while sitting at a table by himself. This program was discussed with his parents who, with Barnie's agreement, were referred to a psychoeducational support group for families to deal with some of the interactional problems they faced when coping with his behaviors.

Barnie became a productive and more confident worker and was gradually able to increase the amount of time spent with his fellow workers. These activities were supplemented by further family sessions that examined how the family could help him to take more responsibility in different areas of his life. Eventually Barnie felt he had mastered both his part-time job and his social contacts in the workplace to the point at which he was ready to attend a short-term community rehabilitation program. This was followed by participation in another rehabilitation program, and finally, 4 years after starting the part-time work program, Barnie found a permanent job working as a janitor.

During this period improvements were noted in Barnie's mood and confidence that enabled him to leave home to live in a supervised boarding home. In his opinion the biggest single change was being paid for work he was doing while in the work group, which enhanced his self-esteem and provided him with his first real "adult world" success since leaving school. Although Barnie continued to require neuroleptic medications, there were no further hospitalizations during this period of his life.

The Physically Disabled

Graham Armstrong was a 38-year-old married father of two who had worked as a truck mechanic for 20 years before being involved in a road accident. The accident resulted in neck injuries that made it impossible for him to continue in his previous job. He referred himself for psychiatric help 2 years after the accident because of feelings of depression and suicidal ideation.

Prior to his accident Mr. and Mrs. Armstrong were planning to move to another part of the country, and Mr. Armstrong had been working up to 70 hours a week to enable the family to buy a house after their move. Following the accident a drawn out claim for compensation and conflicting medical opinions as to his long-term prognosis had left Mr. Armstrong feeling angry and frustrated. His inability to work had had a major impact on the family's financial situation, and their long-term plans had been put on hold. Mr. Armstrong also suffered from a degenerative hearing problem that he felt ruled out the possibility of his obtaining a less physically demanding supervisory position.

When seen for an initial visit Mr. Armstrong described himself as feeling out of control and unable to cope with anything, which was quite alien to his view of himself as an unemotional and controlled individual. He was pessimistic about the likelihood of working again and angry at many people who he thought had let him down or given him bad advice, and he felt badly about not being able to provide adequately for his children. He saw suicide as his only way out.

Impressions

Mr. Armstrong was a well-defended man with long-standing feelings of inferiority in relationships that he had been able to compensate for by his competence at work. The loss of his job, through no fault of his own, had taken away his role as a provider, while the financial hardships had placed additional strain on an already shaky marital relationship.

The physical injury, its medicolegal sequelae, and the uncertainty as to future career prospects had combined to engender in Mr. Armstrong a sense of helplessness and of a loss of control, and had awoken unresolved conflicts about unmet dependency needs.

Interventions

The initial step was to review the various stressors Mr. Armstrong faced, to enable him to differentiate between events that were beyond his control and those that he could do something about. The accident and its consequences and Mr. Armstrong's sense of himself as a helpless victim of circumstances were reviewed and put in a different perspective. His work strengths and assets were emphasized and his work options reviewed. This process provided him with increased hope regarding his future because he realized he had alternatives to simply waiting for the court case to be settled.

The couple were seen together for marital therapy to help them resolve some of the problems they identified. Mr. Armstrong was also seen on a regular basis for psychotherapy that focused on his unresolved dependency conflicts and his reactions when his needs were not met. As his guilt diminished and his anger dissipated, he saw himself less as a victim and felt he could once again take charge of his own destiny. He spent increasing amounts of time with his children and devoted his energy to a job search, with the aid of a counseling program for older workers.

Despite continuing pain, Mr. Armstrong attempted to return to work as a mechanic. When he recognized that he was unable to handle the physical demands of his job, he success-fully applied for a supervisory position with a large haulage firm, without waiting for his claim to be settled. Despite con-cerns about the impact of possible further deterioration in his hearing, Mr. Armstrong's mood and sense of well-being contin-ued to improve, as did the family's financial situation. Eventu-ally, 3 years later than originally planned, the family was able to pay off its debts and move to its new home.

The Single Parent

Sammie Kennedy, a 22-year-old mother of two preschool chil-dren, was referred to a community mental health service for help with symptoms of depression. These symptoms had been present for many years and had worsened over the previous 3 months. Sammie had been pregnant when she married at the age of 17 to escape from an abusive home situation. Her hus-band had numerous affairs during their short-lived relation-ship, drank heavily, and beat her regularly. Three years prior to her referral he had left her, and she had moved into a subsi-dized apartment with her two children. She had never worked, having left school during grade 12 when she got married, and she had few social contacts or supports. Most of her time was spent caring for her children, but limited finances prevented her from being able to afford day-care or baby-sitting that might have provided some relief. Her older son had been iden-tified as having behavioral problems at school, while her daughter had suffered from numerous physical complaints, re-sulting in frequent medical visits.

Sammie presented as feeling anxious and hopeless. She was overwhelmed by her responsibilities and felt her lack of self-esteem and confidence undermined her effectiveness as a parent. She wanted to work but felt she had few skills or assets. Sammie had little idea of how to find suitable work and could not afford a baby-sitter who might facilitate her search for work. Consequently, she spent little time out of her apartment.

Impressions

Sammie was a young woman with long-standing problems with self-esteem who had received little nurturance or recognition while growing up. She had become involved in an unsatisfactory relationship to escape from home, choosing to sacrifice her schooling for the unfulfilled dream of marital security and a role as a mother. Lack of marital support and financial deprivation had increased her isolation, while the demands of her children had made it hard for her to build a support network. Thus there were few personal assets or accomplishments she could identify that might increase her self-esteem.

Interventions

Treatment began with Sammie identifying goals for herself, her family, her social activities, and her work career. She participated in a stress management group for women and was referred to a parent-child drop-in center, where she began to meet other women in similar situations, as well as getting a break from her children.

Subsidized day-care was organized to enable her to return to school to complete grade 12. This was followed by her participation in a work retraining program aimed at single mothers. As her vocational activities increased, she appeared less depressed and anxious, and started to mix socially with other women from the group. She also reestablished contact with her mother, who was prepared to help with baby-sitting. At this point Sammie was seen with her children to examine ways of increasing her competence as a parent.

The retraining program led to work placement and a full-time job, with Sammie continuing her vocational upgrading. Working increased her sense of self-worth and led to the formation of two supportive friendships, which helped her cope with problems that previously had overextended her. There were also significant improvements in her children's behavior and health during this period.

Chapter 8

*The Future:
Implications for Social
Policy and Research*

Chapter 8

The Future: Implications for Social Policy and Research

> You see things; and you say, "why?" But I dream things
> that never were, and I say, "why not?"
>
> George Bernard Shaw *Back to Methuselah*

*I*n many respects the lack of preparedness for the increases in unemployment rates in the early 1980s and the difficulties in developing coordinated and effective interventions are not a surprise. They reflect an absence of consistent, well-integrated strategies for dealing with the problems of those who are unemployed. Of equal concern is the apparent lack of attention being paid to the enormous social upheaval that could result from the changing nature of work. Nowhere is this more evident than in the more established industrialized countries, where the need to plan for the changes brought about by technology, changing patterns of production and distribution, and increased competition from newly industrialized countries should be a priority.

National strategies must address fundamental issues such as what to do about industries that are becoming obsolete, the relationship with newly industrialized nations, the effects of the introduction of new technologies, and the changing expectations regarding the relationship between work and family.

If these issues are to be tackled in a meaningful and productive manner, four steps need to be taken. First, there must be increased public debate on all the issues raised by job loss and work change. This discussion should serve to heighten the awareness of all concerned as to the problems of the unemployed and provide opportunities for solutions or remedies to be explored.

Second, all sections of the community, but especially legislators, must commit themselves to addressing the problem of unemployment. Continued and consistent commitment becomes even more necessary as unemployment levels drop below the "critical" peaks they had reached in the early 1980s. Being unemployed creates problems for millions of North Americans annually and will continue to do so for the foreseeable future.

Third, coordinated and collaborative planning needs to take place at every level of government. Fourth, government, industry, and labor must recognize that social change cannot simply be legislated. Meaningful legislation must be preceded and accompanied by genuine efforts on the part of all involved to ensure that such changes are implemented.

Government Policies

While the responsibilities and accountabilities of national and regional governments will vary, each level of government must develop coordinated strategies for evaluating and alleviating the human impact of economic change. Decisions as to whether there is such a thing as an "acceptable" level of unemployment or whether full employment is an attainable goal are a part of this plan. This should be accompanied by a preparedness to devote additional resources to deal with the problems of unemployment.

In addition to broader economic questions such as the need for possible protective trade legislation, such a plan would have five components:

- Job creation strategies
- Financial support for the unemployed
- Additional social programs

172

- Plant closure legislation
- Employee ownership

Job Creation Strategies

A plan to alleviate unemployment should begin with an appraisal of sectors where jobs are likely to be lost and the development of strategies for creating new jobs and industries. These strategies would allow for regional variation and should be accompanied by appropriate funding and support, with the active participation of all levels of government. Such job creation and retraining programs should provide challenging, long-term job opportunities in both the public and private sectors and should be carefully evaluated to examine the longer-term benefits for those who participate.

Many such programs are proposed but founder because they become political footballs, kicked back and forth between different levels of government, each trying to get maximum credit for a program while contributing the minimum amount of money to support it. A good example of this is the Canadian Government's Program for Older Workers Adjustment (POWA) (Hamilton Spectator 1988). In 1985 the Canadian Employment and Immigration Advisory Council described the problem of older unemployed Canadian workers as an "imminent crisis." The response of the Canadian Government was to announce a new program (POWA), the costs of which were to be shared with participating provincial governments. Over the next 2 years, private negotiations took place to try to convince the participants that they should meet to discuss their respective contributions. However, almost 3 years after the POWA was announced, not a single detail of the program or of its implementation had been made public, nor had a single cent been spent.

Unemployment Benefits

The financial benefits and payments to unemployed people need to be reviewed regularly to ensure that they provide a substantive income. The method by which unemployment benefits are paid should also be examined. In many instances delay in receiving payment or restrictive eligibility criteria create extra hardships for those who are already facing difficulties. Increased portability of pensions, whereby existing pension plans can be transferred to the new workplace, would also assist many laid-off workers.

Financial impediments to the utilization of health and welfare services should be eliminated. Unemployed people have more health problems than working people and often require additional medical treatment. Inadequate insurance coverage, especially for those who are not eligible for welfare, should not force individuals to use their life savings to pay their medical costs.

Additional Social Programs

New social programs are also required, especially to help those who wish to work participate in the labor force. An example of such a program is a coordinated child-care program. Adequate funding should ensure that there is a subsidized space for any child whose parent would otherwise be prohibited from working by the lack of available child-care or by the cost of such care.

The question of early retirement warrants further discussion (Ross 1985; Gordus 1980). This approach could increase the number of available jobs, but it could also cause problems for those who choose to retire. The effects of inflation on pensions that are not index-linked could widen the financial gap between those who are working and those who are retired, and lead to further increases in relative poverty among the elderly.

Legislation

Governments also need to ensure that there is satisfactory legislation to protect workers in plants that are about to close. An example of such legislation is the public law enacted in Janu-

174

ary 1989 in the United States (Public Law 100-379 1988), which requires all workplaces with more than 100 employees to provide at least 60 days notice of an impending closure or mass layoff. While early warning itself has not always proven to be an effective mechanism, it is one important part of a comprehensive strategy, especially when accompanied by local initiatives.

Employee Ownership

One other option to the closure of a plant is for employees of the company or representatives from the local community to take over ownership of the plant and run it as a locally controlled enterprise. This approach may be particularly appropriate for branch plants of larger corporations. Conte (1982) surveyed a number of studies of employee-owned companies and concluded that the average employee-owned company is as profitable as, if not more so than, a privately owned company in the same industry. Reasons for this include improved management, increased turnover, and a lower acceptable level of return on the initial investment.

At the end of 1986, 90% of the 65 employee buyouts in the United States since 1971 were still in business (Rosen et al. 1986). There are specific policies a federal or national government can adopt to facilitate employee buyouts, including federal loan guarantees (as banks are frequently reluctant to finance such ventures) and mandatory prenotification of impending closures (Howland 1988).

Communities

Communities, especially those dependent upon a small number of employers, must develop strategies to diversify their industrial base and prepare contingency plans to deal with the potential loss of a major employer. For smaller communities, advanced warning of a closure (a number of years if possible) can provide an opportunity to develop such a strategy.

Communities can also develop supports and resources for local residents who are trying to cope with the problems of unemployment. These resources may include a crisis line and other support services, the provision of information through booklets, workshops, and prepared kits, the establishment of new programs, and special financial provision for the unemployed to facilitate their participation in social and cultural activities.

One other problem to address is the sense of hopelessness on the part of many schoolchildren, as young as 11 or 12 years old, when they view their prospects of finding work. To counter this sense of hopelessness, there is a need for realistic job preparation and training within the educational system. Increased funding must also be provided for schools in deprived areas to ensure that children with other disadvantages such as being discriminated against because of race or coming from a lower socioeconomic class have every opportunity to develop their potential within the school system (Pierson 1980).

The Workplace

Within the workplace, labor and management both have roles to play, especially if they can look at the problems of unemployed workers collaboratively. It is clearly incumbent upon the employer to provide the maximum possible forewarning of any closure to the work force irrespective of the existence of legislation—especially in smaller plants that may not be covered by any mandatory requirements.

The employer should try to establish retraining or relocation programs, set up information sessions and workshops, provide time off for workers to attend job interviews, and contract with agencies to provide support or counseling to unemployed workers having a hard time managing. If possible, these plans should be organized in conjunction with the local union.

At the same time, organized labor needs to take a more proactive approach to addressing the questions posed by changes in the way we work. For example, alternative approaches to organizing work could be included as a part of contract negotiations or a collective bargaining option, especially if they may lead to the creation of additional jobs. Other issues to include in contractual talks may be worker representation on company boards and increased worker participation in decision making, as well as greater consultation prior to the introduction of new technologies.

Health Services

Health services need to remain aware of the effects of unemployment, predict the problems that may arise, and shift resources to deal with these problems. To achieve this level of responsiveness, medical personnel and health service administrators must be sensitive to the relationship between the loss of a job and an individual's physical and emotional health. This requires an understanding of the ways in which the effects of unemployment are transmitted and an ability to elicit relevant information during an assessment. These skills should be taught during the training of all health professionals, because they will be applicable in many situations that these individuals will encounter on a daily basis in their future careers.

A broader appreciation of the origins of the problems will also further an understanding of the possible roles—and limitations—of the health care system when treating problems that may be social or economic in origin. It is therefore essential for health and mental health services to establish closer working relationships with staff of other community agencies to ensure that unemployed individuals are linked with the most appropriate services when they need them. Agencies need to work together to develop innovative and creative programs to meet the needs of the unemployed. These programs should reflect local conditions and build upon natural supports and resources.

There is a continuing need for public attention and education to be focused on work and job loss and their impact on the emotional well-being of communities. As unemployment levels fall and individuals feel less directly threatened by the prospect of losing their own job, there is a tendency to perceive unemployment as representing a less serious or less severe problem.

While not everyone is likely to experience the problems of unemployment firsthand, each of us will be affected to some degree by other changes in the way we work. Many of these changes are already upon us, and it is essential for psychiatry to play an active role in highlighting the human aspects of these issues as part of what must become a much more lively and productive national debate.

Future Research Directions

Unemployment research has moved beyond the stage of simply documenting the health impacts of job loss and should now be examining more closely specific circumstances that cause or exacerbate problems (Miles 1987). Future research should be focused in the following four general areas.

Characteristics of Individuals and Their Environments

It is important to study the characteristics that highlight those individuals or groups of workers who are at the highest risk of developing emotional problems after losing their job so that subgroups of workers who might benefit from specific interventions can be recognized.

To understand the impact of social and demographic variables it is necessary to design studies to examine the differences in the response to job loss among groups from different cultural or social backgrounds, between men and women, and among workers who have lost their jobs in different ways (e.g., being laid off by plant closures, being fired, or choosing to leave). Studies with a uniform design but either conducted in different communities or conducted in one community with different target groups of unemployed workers would provide some insight into the role of these variables.

The Future: Implications for Social Policy and Research

Characteristics of Family and Social Supports

Research into family and social supports should follow two directions. The first is to continue the recent trend of looking more closely at specific characteristics of an individual's family or social support system that can affect the outcome of losing a job. For example, recent research on social support has clarified specific functions of a support system, highlighted the importance of attitudes toward working, and looked at the support needs of different individuals.

A similar approach should be taken with family functions so that characteristics of supportive or destructive families can be identified. This identification will then lead to more specific interventions aimed at different aspects of the worker's social milieu. It will also help further our understanding of the concept of the "fit" between a person and his or her environment.

The second direction for research is to examine the impact of job loss on the spouses and children of unemployed workers, especially those who have been out of work for a year or longer. In particular, greater attention should be paid to the effects of unemployment on the physical and emotional health and behavior of the children of those who lose their jobs, and the ways in which this experience of unemployment might color these children's attitudes toward working or their own future career prospects.

Ways Problems Develop and Moderating Factors

Recognizing that many overlapping or interconnected factors can lead to the development of emotional problems when a job is lost, it is essential to look at the interactions of these factors to further understand how the presence of one can alter, magnify, or nullify the effect of another. Future research must examine in more detail the ways in which these interactions occur. It must also look at which combinations of factors are most likely to protect an individual or expose him or her to the most distressing consequences of losing a job. It will also be

179

important to examine how these factors change as the period of unemployment lengthens, and the social and economic implications these changes might have.

Outcome research can be more accurate if fuller preunemployment profiles of an individual's psychological well-being and family and social functioning can be developed. The use of different screening instruments in these studies, such as the Diagnostic Interview Schedule or the Schedule for Affective Disorders and Schizophrenia, may clarify the role of unemployment in the development of major psychiatric disorders.

Evaluation of Clinical and Preventive Interventions

A fourth area for future research should be the evaluation of interventions with the unemployed. This evaluation encompasses preventive, treatment, and postunemployment community programs. It is necessary to know whether interventions are effective, efficient, and efficacious, as well as to identify who utilizes such programs. If those who are at greatest risk or who could benefit the most from new programs are not being reached, different approaches will be required.

As scientific investigation broadens our understanding of the relationship between mental health problems and unemployment, new theories and hypotheses will evolve, which will in turn need to be tested. We believe the model proposed in this book provides a conceptual basis for such studies that can in turn be adapted as research in the field progresses and our understanding increases.

References

Conte M: Participation and performance in U.S. labor managed firms, in Participatory and Self-Managed Firms. Edited by Jones D, Svenjar J. Lexington, MA, Lexington Books, 1982, pp 213–237

Gordus JP: Leaving Early: Perspectives and Problems in Current Retirement Practice and Policy. Kalamazoo, MI, WE Upjohn Institute for Employment Research, 1980

Hamilton Spectator, Aug 20, 1988, A7

Howland M: Plant Closings and Worker Displacement. Kalamazoo, MI, WE Upjohn Institute for Employment Research, 1988

Miles I: Some observations on "unemployment and health" research. Soc Sci Med 25:223–226, 1987

Pierson F: The Minimum Level of Unemployment and Public Policy. Kalamazoo, MI, WE Upjohn Institute for Employment Research, 1980

Public Law No 100-379: Worker Adjustment and Retraining Notification Act, 1988

Rosen C, Klein K, Young K: Employee Ownership in America: The Equity Solution. Lexington, MA, Lexington Books, 1986

Ross M (ed): The Economics of Aging. Kalamazoo, MI, WE Upjohn Institute for Employment Research, 1985

Chapter 9

Summary

Chapter 9

Summary

> Overall, it is only when you lodge in streets where no-body has a job, where getting a job seems about as possible as owning an aeroplane, that you begin to grasp the changes that are being wrought in our civilisation.
>
> George Orwell *The Road to Wigan Pier*

*I*t is possible that no single activity defines adulthood more specifically than work. To a large extent work influences how and where an individual lives, it affects social contacts and family activities, and it provides a title, role, and environment that shape or reinforce an individual's identity (Group for the Advancement of Psychiatry 1982).

The majority of workers will be faced with a period of unemployment at some time during their life. While some will cope with the stress and problems created by job loss with a minimum of disruption, a large number of workers will find the effects to be traumatic and painful, and many will find their lives changed irrevocably.

Unemployment has been an important social issue since the 1930s and must remain so today, as millions of North Americans who wish to work remain without jobs. We need to recognize, however, that the factors that contribute to unemployment and the problems faced by the jobless are continually changing. We are also embarking on an era of profound change in the way we work. Economic changes, technological advances, new social roles for women, and an increasing proportion of older citizens will all have an impact on the way work is organized, and each may contribute to the disappearance of jobs.

Although new jobs are being created, many of these are in the service sector and are characterized by low pay, little security, and limited benefits. In contrast, many of the disappearing jobs, particularly in the manufacturing sector, are well paying, offer both security and opportunities for career advancement, and require higher levels of education for workers wishing to enter the field.

The net result of these changes has been the solidification of a two-tier work force. A smaller percentage of workers are acquiring a greater proportion of the good jobs, while an increasing percentage of the population—often those with other social disadvantages—face the prospect of increasingly limited work opportunities. There is also a group of "hard-core" unemployed, who, for reasons that are often beyond their control, may be excluded from the work force permanently. The development of such a disadvantaged and alienated underclass, whose attitudes toward work and society are often pessimistic or hopeless even before leaving school, will have serious long-term consequences.

Although up to 15% of the population will experience a period of unemployment each year, surprisingly few well-designed studies of the psychological effects of unemployment have been reported in the psychiatric literature. Methodological differences and the complexity of the ways that losing a job can have an impact have resulted in some apparently contradictory findings. This is particularly the case with the question of the extent to which unemployment creates new emotional difficulties, exposes preexisting problems, or adds to already stressful social circumstances that in turn lead to the development or exacerbation of problems.

Two conclusions can be drawn from this debate. First, each of the proposed schema is probably applicable in certain cases, and in many situations all are relevant. There is sufficient evidence that job loss, whether on its own or in combination with other factors, does lead to significant changes in the well-being of individuals and their families.

Second, it is vital to recognize that the factors that influence the outcome of a period of unemployment are in a dynamic interrelationship. Their effects can be cumulative, but the presence of one can sometimes prevent or modify the impact of others. Appreciating the complexity of these interactions and the impact they can have on an individual is crucial to the development of a comprehensive intervention strategy.

Previous studies have demonstrated consistently that the loss of a job leads to a reduced sense of self-confidence or personal effectiveness and causes symptoms of emotional distress in both the unemployed and their family members. There is less evidence regarding its role in the development of major psychiatric disorders. As time passes, it is likely that factors that are secondary to job loss play an increasingly prominent role in the development or maintenance of emotional problems. Again, variables such as the meaning the job may have had for the worker and the degree of financial deprivation will influence the way an individual copes and the nature of the difficulties he or she may encounter.

When assessing the problems of an unemployed individual, therefore, mental health workers must be aware of the kinds of problems likely to be encountered. Issues commonly faced include difficulties in dealing with the losses, decreased self-esteem, reduction in social support, changes in roles and family relationships, increased stress, and an uncovering of preexisting problems.

An assessment should be comprehensive, involving other family members or important supports whenever possible. In addition to reviewing the effects of losing a job or remaining unemployed on the individual and his or her family, it is also important to examine personal strengths and deficits that may have predated the loss of the job. Changes in social routines and the availability of support are important, but perceptions of changes in these areas may have even more of an impact than the changes themselves.

Many of the unemployed who develop emotional problems do not come into contact with mental health services. They may see little relevance in psychiatric help, particularly for what they may perceive as practical problems, or they may be deterred by the cost of any treatment. For many, especially those with milder symptoms, psychotropic medication or psychotherapy may not be appropriate treatments. Many of the unemployed will, however, be in regular contact with their family physician or staff of other community agencies.

To be able to intervene successfully, therefore, psychiatric services must be able to offer a broad range of interventions that include consultation, public education, prevention, and collaboration with community agencies, as well as more traditional treatments for individuals and their families. This can only be achieved if mental health workers are able to take a systemic or ecological view of the impact of job loss and can establish links with other community agencies that may be in a better position to provide necessary services. A knowledge of available community resources is therefore essential for a therapist dealing with unemployed workers.

Unemployment develops in a wide socioeconomic context. Accordingly, efforts at a local level need to reinforce, and be reinforced by, policies formulated at national and regional levels. Governments, industry, and labor must start planning for the possible effects of economic, technological, and social change on the work force so that long-term job strategies can be developed and necessary adjustments made. This action requires political will and a commitment of resources.

Experiences over the last decade have not been promising. The debate about unemployment remains dominated by impersonal statistics. Unless there is increased public awareness of the human cost of being without work, and acceptance of the belief that each citizen has a right to meaningful employment, reflected in economic and social planning, millions of North Americans will continue to experience the distressing and frequently debilitating sequelae of losing a job. This is a problem that society in general and psychiatry in particular cannot and must not ignore.

Reference

Group for the Advancement of Psychiatry: Job Loss—A Psychiatric Perspective. New York, Mental Health Materials Center, 1982